Apocalypse Ready

Apocalypse Ready

The Manual of Manuals
A Century of Panic Prevention

Taras Young

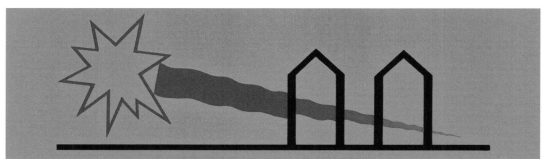

Contents

Introduction 6

① Pandemic 20
Tuberculosis 26
Spanish Flu 44
Asian Flu and Hong Kong Flu 54
HIV/AIDS 60
Recent Viruses 66
② Natural Disaster 74
Extreme Weather 82
When the Earth Moves 102
Fighting Fire 126
Survive in the Wild 140
③ Nuclear War 152
Preparation 160
Shelter 174
Blast and Fallout 186
④ Alien Invasion 216
We Come in Peace 220
Is There Anyone Out There? 234
What Is the Truth? 240

Resources 250
Sources 252
Index 254
Acknowledgments 256

A note on the captioning in this book:
❶ A solid caption number presents information taken from the original source material.
① A hollow caption number presents new, explanatory information.

Introduction

Cataclysms of one sort or another perpetually lurk in the darkest regions of our minds. We tell ourselves that the chance of a global-scale catastrophe actually happening to *us* is small. Yet, in idle moments, many of us think about what we would do – how we would feel, how we would act – should the very worst happen. Would you trust your instincts to save your life and the lives of those you love? Could you look up at a nuclear mushroom cloud and know the best course of action? Would you know the warning signs of a tsunami? And how would you really react if aliens landed on your street tomorrow?

Throughout the 20th century, a variety of forces posed enormous threats to global civilization that were out of all human control. They ranged in scope from natural disasters – which, while we would never wish to experience them, we could at least comprehend – to the completely inconceivable threat of global thermonuclear war. In these situations, our first line of defence – in some cases, our only line of defence – was to know how to act should the worst happen.

This was the century in which rapid globalization saw the world become more interconnected and more interdependent than ever before.

As it became significantly easier and cheaper to travel around the globe, pandemic diseases hitched a ride along with us, claiming millions of lives. In 1918, the Spanish flu took advantage of a vulnerable, war-weary world, travelling with troops and plotting a deadly course from country to country. Some 40 years later, disease struck again as the Asian flu pandemic gripped the planet, returning in waves year after year for more than a decade, before eventually mutating into the Hong Kong flu pandemic of 1968. In the 1980s, the emergence of HIV/AIDS presented a frightening new type of pandemic for which science was ill-prepared.

For public health officials, information became a critical tool in helping to combat pandemics. Materials advising the public on actions they could take, and habits they could break, were a primary defence against the spread of disease.

In this century, the insignificance of the human race continued to be underscored, as it had been for millennia, by the untameable forces of nature. Earthquakes, volcanoes and extreme weather impacted lives around the world. However, progress in understanding the forces involved, improved communications channels and increasingly refined monitoring

① Cataclysm is a human preoccupation. This scene from the disaster movie *Tidal Wave* (1973) shows Japan being inundated by water.

Pages 8–17: images and quotes taken from *Personal Protection Under Atomic Attack*, Civil Defence Canada, 1951.

①

and warning systems meant that people could predict and mitigate the effects of these events better than ever before. Here, too, arming the public with information on how to behave led to lives being saved. Furthermore, government-sponsored research into how people react in natural disaster areas helped to improve the way life-saving information was presented. However, the latter years of the 20th century saw a new environmental threat emerge in the form of man-made climate change.

The second half of the century was also dogged by the enormous threat of nuclear annihilation. Although the threat was constant, its perceived severity waxed and waned depending on the political climate. During a period of unsettled 'peace', the Cold War saw

East and West held in a chronic stalemate, interspersed with proxy wars such as those in Vietnam (1955–75) and Korea (1950–53). The world was pushed to the very brink of destruction by global near misses, such as the Cuban Missile Crisis in 1962 and the lesser-known Able Archer war scare in 1983, during the latter of which Soviet commanders misinterpreted a Western war game as cover for a nuclear first strike.

People around the world found themselves prisoners of the principle of nuclear deterrence – the belief that the other side would not attack first, as it would spell the end for humanity – and characterized it as 'mutually assured destruction', or MAD. It gradually became clear that there could be no winner in a nuclear conflict,

'The apartment dweller... is responsible firstly for his own family'

and no defence against nuclear weapons. Once the chain reaction of retaliatory strikes began, the world would be destroyed forever: it was often said that after a nuclear war, the living would envy the dead. However, governments tried to stay upbeat, and public guidance on how to cope with life under fallout conditions was created and distributed on both sides of the conflict.

Finally, scientific breakthroughs led to the development of new technologies at a considerable rate, propelling humans into space for the first time. People increasingly looked to the stars and wondered whether we were alone in the universe – and, if we were not, who else was out there. Claims of alien sightings, encounters and even abductions began to invade the pages of daily newspapers, and creatures from outer space fast became staples of popular culture. This brought to mind another threat: that of invasion, not by another country, but by beings from other worlds (although, arguably, one was a psychological stand-in for the other). It is hard to say how much serious thought governments gave to preparing the public to deal with the alien threat. But – perhaps surprisingly – we do know that UFOs were seen as

a real threat to national security. From the 1950s to the end of the century, administrations around the world invested significant time and money in gathering, analysing and trying to make sense of data on the alleged spacecraft.

A holiday from history
It is clear, then, that the 20th century was a period in which the world was persistently on the verge of experiencing one cataclysm or another. The exception was the final few years of the century. For those who grew up in the 1990s, threats such as a nuclear attack or a global pandemic seemed as outlandish as that of an extraterrestrial visitation. Indeed, the decade is now becoming recognized as something of a historical anomaly: for many in the industrialized Western world, it was a time characterized by relative peace, progress and prosperity. With the break-up of the Soviet Union, the perceived threat of nuclear attack, which had been in place for some 40 years, lifted. Advances in medicine kept more infectious diseases under control than ever before, and new technology meant the detection and management of natural disasters was sounder than it had ever been. Best of all, the alien invasion that had been threatened by endless Hollywood B-movies had failed to materialize – despite the insistence of those who had observed alien craft – silver discs, cigar-shaped objects and black triangles – hovering in the skies, or had experienced close encounters of their own.

'If you are caught out of doors when the flash comes, drop to the ground'

This lack of major global upheavals following the collapose of the Soviet Union has led to the 1990s being described as a 'holiday from history'. Like all holidays, though, it had to come to an end. With the tragedy of the terrorist attacks on the United States in 2001, the 21st century was set up for a return to the world's 'normal' state of international turmoil, disorder and general peril.

Readers of this book are likely to have had first-hand experience of a global-level cataclysm, although it may not yet have fully sunk in. The COVID-19 pandemic has left an indelible impact on humanity, with no nation or individual unaffected in some way. At the time of writing, COVID-19 has already had a far greater impact than either Asian flu or Hong Kong flu, the 20th century's two 'forgotten' pandemics. In terms of scale, it has more in common with the Spanish flu, which gripped the world a hundred years prior. The COVID-19 pandemic has changed the way we live and work; it has killed millions and reduced the quality of life for many millions more; and it has ravaged economies around the world. Given the giant leaps that scientists made in our understanding of virology during the 20th century, COVID-19 would undoubtedly have

been very much worse had it occurred a century earlier.

We are yet to fully appreciate the long-term political and social consequences of this pandemic, but it seems likely that they will be enormous. While some aspects of the global response to COVID-19 – such as the rapid development not only of new vaccines, but new types of vaccine – have been rightly lauded, the response of most governments has been at best clumsy and at worst criminal. And yet, pandemics are just one of the unthinkable calamities that can become a reality in the blink of an eye.

Our flawed human intuition
The chances of a catastrophic event may be small, but knowing what to do when things go awry can mean the difference between life and death. Our ability to survive cataclysms is hampered by the simple fact that they are infrequent; human intuition is not equipped to deal with unusual disasters, and nobody believes that such an event will happen to them. This means that how we act when faced with a catastrophe is often at odds with how we *should* act. Our automatic reaction to unimaginable and unlikely events can even be counterproductive; human nature gets in the way and makes situations worse. One example can be seen in videos of the Boxing Day tsunami of 2004: people watch curiously as the Indian Ocean rapidly draws back from the shore in what must have

'Keep any valuable papers you may have around the house in a fireproof metal box'

been an astonishing, otherworldly sight. However, the correct response, the counterintuitive one, is to run in the opposite direction as quickly as possible. Advice on how to prepare for catastrophes must address this type of cognitive bias.

Given the enormous economic, social and environmental damage a global-scale catastrophe can cause, it makes sense for those in power to do everything they can to prepare people for a variety of worst-case scenarios. Ever-improving living conditions in the 20th century led to a worldwide population boom. Together with the widening of the franchise in established democracies and the spread of communism in other places, governments – more than ever before – found themselves accountable for what befell their people. Massive disasters, of course, can also impact the state's ability to function, and – if they are handled badly – its legitimacy. It has been claimed that any society is only ever four meals away from anarchy; any disaster massive enough to injure a sufficient proportion of the populace will also inevitably damage the state. Thus, it is deeply in the interest of any government to ensure that its people are well-prepared, not only from

a humanitarian point of view, but also in terms of maintaining its own integrity.

To that end, the century saw a new focus on informing, educating and preparing the public for disaster. For each potential catastrophe identified, governments set about developing materials to help people help themselves, their families and their neighbours. In the early part of the century, public information initially took the form of printed matter: posters, advertisements and booklets. Keeping pace with technology, this grew to include broadcast media in the form of radio and television, and, towards the end of the century, the Internet.

Informing the people

So how do you go about giving people advice? The effectiveness of disaster preparedness materials depends on several factors. Public information must take into account audience literacy. The greater the number of people who can understand and carry out the instructions, the more useful the information will be. However, this must be balanced with the value of the guidance itself: there is no point making advice simple to follow if it also makes it significantly less effective. It is here that the development of new communication media played an important part. The show-and-tell nature of broadcast media in the 20th century gave government public information experts exciting new ways to inform the public. Radio and television

'It is essential to have an organized control system'

certainly had the edge over printed materials for their sheer accessibility: they exposed people to information passively, rather than requiring them to make the effort to read something. However, before the advent of mobile phones and on-demand media, printed materials were still key; you could not carry an instructional video in your pocket, ready to consult should disaster strike.

Public information campaigns in the latter half of the 20th century began to share a significant proportion of their DNA with integrated commercial advertising campaigns for consumer products. Officials realized that selling disaster advice was not so far removed from selling a washing machine.

While a booklet or radio broadcast on its own could be somewhat effective, pairing up different modes of communication could substantially increase the chance of messages being remembered and understood. By combining printed booklets, newspaper advertisements, television broadcasts and radio spots, public information campaigns could hit people from different angles. This was particularly the case with campaigns around the threat of global thermo-nuclear war – a universal, realistic

and persistent danger that warranted significant official investment to prepare the public. As a result, several multichannel public education campaigns were created, such as 'Duck and Cover' in the United States in the 1950s and 'Protect and Survive' in the United Kingdom in the 1970s. The latter programme comprised a series of animated films that were to be broadcast on all television channels on loop ahead of an anticipated nuclear attack, plus instructional radio spots, newspaper advertisements and simple, authoritative yet attractive illustrated booklets that would be dropped onto the doormat of every household.

Any one of these approaches on its own would have been useful, but together they provided a more powerful campaign. Hearing instructions on the radio, seeing them acted out on television and receiving a booklet in the post would reinforce the advice and make sure the greatest number of people absorbed it fully.

Creating advice that works
Over the course of the 20th century, successive governments developed and refined the ways in which they communicate disaster advice to their people. A wide range of factors governs how ordinary people respond to official advice about unthinkable threats. The advice must be easy to follow, with a clear reason or goal to achieve. You cannot simply throw together a set of instructions and expect citizens to understand and remember them in a time of crisis.

'While speed is essential, don't start a mad rush which could cause panic'

In order to compile the right advice, governments drew on a diverse range of disciplines, including psychology, sociology, public relations and disaster management, to try to establish the most effective ways of getting the message across. Disaster guidance moved away from text-heavy tomes towards simplified instructions. For example, in the 1950s, nuclear attack guides went into great detail, explaining the mechanics of nuclear weapons and describing plans for constructing different types of fallout shelter. By the 1980s, much of this detail had been pared back, leaving only the step-by-step actions a typical citizen would need to take.

Indeed, the quality and presentation of information is key. Design choices such as typography, iconography and illustrations can play a significant role in communicating official information in a way that ensures it is retained. Putting effort into the presentation of materials is essential: attractive, well-designed pamphlets are kept, whereas poorly designed ones are discarded. Emergency planning information can be imbued with authority by using typefaces or symbols typically associated with the state or government, further ensuring that information is retained

and trusted. Once a crisis hits, a clearly laid-out poster or booklet could make the difference between someone taking the correct action to save lives or making mistakes – or ignoring the advice altogether.

By paying attention to the design and layout of printed materials, officials can ensure that guidance will be easy to understand and easy to act on. It is wrong to assume that officials are capable of meeting these criteria without support. In 1980, prior to the construction of the Thames Barrier, the Greater London Council (GLC) was deeply concerned with the problem of the River Thames flooding. The river had come dangerously close to bursting its banks in 1965, 1975 and 1978; had it done so, some 116 sq km (45 sq mi) of the city would have been put at risk, including 20,000 homes, 50 London Underground stations and 35 hospitals. It was vital that citizens knew what to do should the flood warnings sound. The GLC enlisted the help of a graphic designer to assess the various London boroughs' disaster preparedness materials. As well as numerous inconsistencies in the advice given by different local authorities, he found that much of the literature contained flaws, including overlong sentences and decorative illustrations that added no practical value to the guidance. The choice of cover photographs was also an issue: some of them simply showed a high tide, severely underplaying the catastrophic consequences of a real London flood. With a more impactful design,

'If you can avoid it, don't leave the car at the curb since the blast might blow it into the middle of the road'

people would be more likely to accept the risk and be prepared to act on it.

Human behaviour and risk perception

Being able to predict how people will view official advice, whether they will trust its authority and ultimately how they will act on it in a crisis is vital for those tasked with creating emergency information. Trust in a government's authority when issuing advice around preparing for catastrophes is a particularly significant factor. How the message is delivered, and who is delivering it, really makes a difference. If the reader does not believe that the instructions they have been given are correct, then those instructions are worse than useless because they will cause a wider erosion of trust in official advice across the board. It is, therefore, important that government communicators do everything in their power to ensure that the emergency guidance they create is trusted – particularly where the correct course of action is counterintuitive or difficult to explain succinctly.

For this reason, governments have commissioned academic studies and market research as part of their ongoing disaster planning activities.

Research by risk management specialists into behavioural responses to flood and earthquake warnings, for example, has helped to define how warning systems are designed and how threats are communicated. Focus groups are also used to understand how people might interpret and react to advice on dealing with disaster. In the 1980s, the UK government rigorously tested nuclear war survival information with panels comprising ordinary members of the public. They checked whether the average citizen would understand key emergency instructions, such as building a fallout shelter, and also gauged their views on television and radio commercials that would be broadcast if an attack was imminent. They then adjusted the official advice accordingly.

Popular culture has a role to play in how we interpret government information, too. For example, movies allow us to imagine how a disaster might play out without having to experience it for ourselves. Hollywood has tackled every kind of cataclysm, from pandemics (*Contagion*, *World War Z*, *I Am Legend*) to nuclear war (*Threads*, *The Day After*, *Dr. Strangelove*), natural disasters (*Twister*, *Supervolcano*, *The Wizard of Oz*) and alien invasion (too many to mention). The depiction of cataclysms on screen can help to prepare the public for the real thing: they allow audiences to face their fears in a safe environment, think about how they would act in the same situation and discuss the scenario with others. However, movies can also have a

detrimental effect on the public's perception of risk. For example, tornados are almost universally depicted as taking place in rural locations, but in reality they can occur anywhere.

The fact that our heroes frequently survive, despite the odds, also serves to downplay the risk involved in major disasters. It plays into a human flaw, a cognitive bias, that is a key problem with which emergency planners are familiar. Known as 'normalcy bias', it is a psychological quirk that creates a period of initial disbelief or denial during a time of extreme crisis, thereby causing people to fail to appreciate the danger they are in and to fail to act appropriately. It is what leads people to gather at the beach and stare out to sea moments before a tsunami; it is why we do not evacuate as a volcano is erupting, and why many of us ignore flood and tornado warnings. This underestimation of risk has been found to lead to less obvious consequences during natural disasters, too. Studies in the United States and in France have found that, during severe flooding, male drivers take particularly dangerous and inappropriate actions, such as attempting to drive through the water. In fact, more than half of all flood deaths in the United States are drivers who have made poor decisions.

At Armero in Colombia, normalcy bias combined with a lack of public and official trust in the advice of disaster preparedness experts led directly to a tremendous loss of life. Armero lay 48 km (30 mi) from the Nevado del Ruiz volcano. Scientists and civil defence organizations had warned that the town was in critical danger of flooding should the volcano erupt, even going so far as to distribute maps showing the path of the floods. Their warnings were dismissed as scaremongering by the government. On 13 November 1985, when Nevado del Ruiz erupted, the government and residents went about their business as ash rained down on the town. Meanwhile, the eruption was melting glaciers on the volcano. These soon caused massive mud flows to engulf the town, killing more than 20,000 people – two-thirds of Armero's population. After the tragedy, cities across Colombia began to focus on disaster planning programmes, thus showing that sometimes it takes direct experience of a catastrophe to ensure that risks are taken seriously.

A healthier state of affairs exists in Mexico City, where a study has investigated the perceived threat from Popocatépetl, an active volcano located 70 km (43 mi) from the city. It found that concern about the danger from the volcano increased depending on the official alert level (a fairly abstract concept with only three possible levels). When officials raised the alert level, people's

'There is no
need to alarm
the youngsters'

perception of risk from the volcano increased and they were more likely to take action, even though there was no obvious change in daily life.

The idea that more abstract guidance makes people pay more attention to major risks is supported by research carried out in the United Kingdom, which looked at how people behave when receiving flood warnings. Somewhat counterintuitively, the study found that the best way to ensure people are informed about risks to life and property was not to make specific claims or statements, but rather to issue materials that create a climate of uncertainty and provide simple answers to questions. The uncertainty created by this approach leads to the public informally educating themselves on the risk, and also discussing it with family, friends and neighbours. This, in turn, leads to a better-prepared, better-informed and more risk-aware community.

Another way to make sure people do not ignore cataclysmic threats is to engage in 'consequence-based messaging'. Researchers in the United States investigating how tornado warnings are interpreted found that many ordinary people struggle to identify risks in traditional, probability-based messages, which simply state the likelihood of a tornado touching down in their area. While some correctly interpreted warnings and headed for shelter, or took other protective actions, others simply accepted the message and carried on as before, in some cases with tragic outcomes. The researchers found that introducing consequences into tornado warnings alongside probabilities – for example, 'You could be killed if you are not underground or in a tornado shelter' – increased the chances of people taking life-saving action.

Political ideology and emergency guidance
Every country has its own culture and ideology, meaning that each government communicates with its people differently. This has led to a variety of approaches to informing the public, based on differing national cultures and the political leanings of those in power. If we look at the imagery and advice given in 20th-century emergency planning materials, they are often broadly aligned with the prevailing ideologies of the governments that created them.

Those designed by Western democracies tended to focus on the individual and the actions they could take to protect themselves, their immediate family and their property. Evidence of the state was minimal or absent; illustrations frequently depicted one person taking action on their own, or at most as part of a small family unit. Common advice was to stay in your own home, build

'The ground burst... would shake its surroundings like a minature earthquake'

your own shelter and prepare for your own survival. Materials produced in socialist countries focused instead on community safety and survival, depicting people outside, working together for the greater good. They were far more likely to involve representations of state aid at a time of crisis, such as doctors and nurses offering medical assistance to their fellow citizens, and members of the military working together with ordinary people to shore up defences.

To those raised in liberal democracies, materials produced by communist countries can seem propaganda-like in tone. Of course, this is partly because the approach to official communications in communist countries differs significantly from that of capitalist societies, where imbuing official advice with dogma would be immediately questioned or ridiculed. However, it is useful to view all public information issued by any government as propaganda, regardless of where or when it was produced. For example, it is questionable whether public information advice around nuclear war would actually have been of real practical use had it ever been needed. The advice given in the West, with its focus on the individual and the family, has been interpreted by some as a way

of keeping ordinary citizens distracted while ensuring the continuity of the state. While the people were busy thinking about stocking their larders or constructing ramshackle fallout shelters in their homes, they would not be destabilizing the government through mass protests or blocking the military from using key transport routes by trying to evacuate cities. Even if governments were not directly thinking in this way, there is a further question of whether government preparation for unimaginable disasters is more a case of being 'seen' to be doing something rather than actually offering useful advice. People want to be reassured that their government is doing all it can to ready the nation for a crisis, so the act of creating materials itself becomes a political act. For the domestic audience, official readiness allays fears that the government would lose control in a crisis; to a foreign audience, preparedness can be a sign of strength.

Of course, this depends on the materials being seen as valid. One way to ensure this is to advertise their existence without releasing the materials themselves. The United Kingdom's 'Protect and Survive' programme on surviving a nuclear attack is a case in point. It was prepared in the 1970s, and there was some vague public awareness that the campaign existed, but it was carefully designed to retain its potency by being held back until an attack seemed imminent. When the Conservative government led by Margaret Thatcher came to power

'If you follow certain rules, there is no need to fear danger from radioactivity in food and drink'

in 1979, the nuclear advice materials were leaked to the establishment media, and soon after they were made officially available to the public. This backfired dramatically. The widespread derision that followed the release turned the campaign into a laughing stock. It ensured that the information could never be taken seriously by the public and gave anti-nuclear campaigners an endless source of material with which to mock the government's position.

To this day, public information campaigns issued by the UK govern-ment find themselves the subject of unfavourable comparisons with 'Protect and Survive', underlining how one false step can undermine public trust for many years.

Nationalism and cultural identity

It is also possible for governments to portray the state as something to be protected, by bringing notions of nationalism and patriotism into play. In this case, a person can be convinced that they must play their part in order to ensure the survival of the state or culture with which they personally identify. Civil defence posters from socialist Hungary, for example, show people from all walks of life standing together to support the protection of the nation. Cultural identity can also be seen at play in the form of traditional colours and symbolism being used on AIDS campaign posters in Zimbabwe, and in safe sex posters designed to target Aboriginal communities in Australia.

Of course, there is also a less palatable side to playing on people's national or cultural identity in this way. The Spanish flu, Asian flu and Hong Kong flu pandemics became associated with the places they supposedly originated, regardless of how accurate this was. A billboard campaign that appeared during the Hong Kong flu pandemic in the late 1960s claimed that 'Hong Kong flu is Un-American' and advised people to 'catch something made in the USA'. Associating a disease with another country or cultural identity is nothing new: syphilis was historically known as the 'French disease' by the British, the 'Neapolitan disease' by the French, the 'Polish disease' by the Russians and the 'German disease' by the Poles. Later, the false assumption that HIV/AIDS was linked directly to homosexual activity led to a slow response by public health authorities, which only served to deepen the crisis.

Disaster preparedness materials in the 20th century largely failed to consider that they should cater to a diverse audience. Usually, one version of official guidance was produced to meet the needs of the majority of people. In countries such as the United Kingdom, Canada and the United States, this often meant a focus on the experiences of white, English-speaking, suburban, middle-class homeowners. While this laser focus doubtless reflected those involved in creating the materials, failing to cater to certain groups inevitably results in a less well-prepared population.

One problem with this approach is that it is difficult, or even impossible, to follow advice that simply does not apply to your circumstances. For example, how do you build a fallout shelter in your garden when you live in a tower block? How do you move to the safety of a higher floor when you live in a caravan? Another issue is that of representation: if nobody in the materials looks like you, the chance that you will connect with the guidance and take it seriously is reduced. Finally, if you cannot access the advice in the first place, you have no chance of understanding and acting on it. This last point, at least, had started to be addressed by the end of the century. Governments began to evolve the variants of each public information campaign, creating versions in multiple languages. In the United Kingdom, information is now routinely provided in Braille, as audio recordings and as specially produced sign language videos. In Japan, earthquake advice is created in multiple languages across print and broadcast media, in order to ensure that everyone has access to an equal chance of survival.

A century of panic prevention
Following advice can be difficult – doubly so when your life may depend on it. Throughout the 20th century, governments around the world worked hard to find effective ways of communicating risk, preparing people for unimaginable threats and providing guidance on how to survive various disasters.

Humanity has faced many cataclysms, some as old as time: earthquakes, volcanic eruptions, extreme weather and pandemic disease. Great leaps forward in technology have also left humanity staring into new abysses in the form of nuclear war and climate change. Meanwhile, our first voyages into space have meant confronting our universal insignificance, inviting alien beings to haunt our thoughts. But the same technological advances that have created new risks have also led to new ways of preventing them. Breakthrough technologies such as radio, television and the Internet have democratized information and made it easier for governments to share advice. Research by psychologists, sociologists, designers and emergency planners has provided new insights into human behaviour and allowed information to be tailored and presented in ways that ensure it is ever more useful.

Apocalypse Ready is a record of government advice in the first information age. It brings together our best efforts at using communication to help society face the unthinkable.

② Superior beings from Mars make light work of Earth's defences in *The War of the Worlds* (1953).
③ Cities slide into the sea in *2012* (2009), a disaster movie based on the mistaken premise that the world would end in that year.

②

③

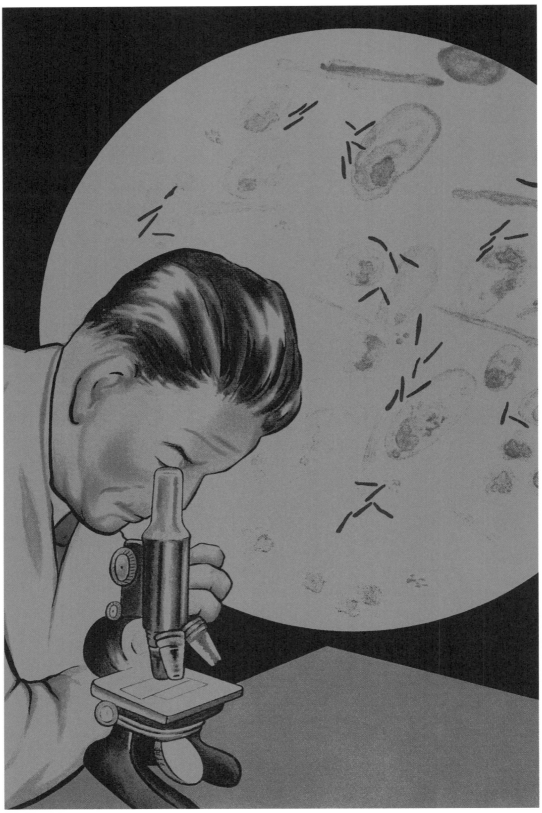

Pandemic

Tuberculosis	26
Spanish Flu	44
Asian Flu and Hong Kong Flu	54
HIV/AIDS	60
Recent Viruses	66

①

1. Pandemic

Don't Die of Ignorance*
Preparing for Pandemics

* 'AIDS: Don't Die of Ignorance' was a public health campaign launched in 1986 by the UK government in response to the HIV/AIDS pandemic. The campaign included leaflets and television advertisements, which today are remembered for their apocalyptic tone and dramatic imagery, including a volcano, iceberg and tombstone.

① *Protect Mankind with the Early Diagnosis of Pulmonary Tuberculosis – Don't Delay!* (*Prevenire il male per la diagnosi precoce della tubercolosi polmonare – niente paura!*), Italy, 1936. One of a series of three Fascist-era public health postcards; the reverse offers advice on preventing tuberculosis.

Humanity has endured pandemics for many thousands of years. The great historical plagues that eviscerated medieval populations were undoubtedly pandemics in the modern sense. In the 6th century, the Plague of Justinian was the catalyst for what is now called the 'first plague pandemic', which returned at least 15 times over the subsequent 200 years. Perhaps more familiar is the Black Death, the 14th-century outbreak of bubonic plague, which retains the record as the deadliest pandemic of all time: waves of pestilence wiped out at least 30 per cent – and perhaps as much as 60 per cent – of the entire human population. It triggered a second plague pandemic – altering history and dramatically setting back global development in the process – which lasted in some places until the early 1700s. Of course, plague is but one example of deadly disease; humanity has been in a protracted battle throughout time with others such as influenza, typhus and cholera.

The concept of the 'pandemic', however, is itself a relatively modern creation. It first entered currency in the late 19th century, thanks to an increasing interest in using statistics to quantify the impact of disease. With this development, governments began to think they could objectively monitor and understand how pandemics spread. As a result, they began to create guidance on how people should behave in order to curb their transmission and impact on public health.

The 20th century – like every century before it – hosted a series of pandemics. However, several major changes affected the spread and reach of contagious diseases. Over the course of a hundred years, the global population leapt from below 2 billion to more than 6 billion. At the same time, international travel became cheaper, faster and more commonplace, giving bacteria and viruses more opportunities to hitch a ride. In humanity's favour, many parts of the world saw standards of living dramatically improve, and advances in medical science led to a deeper understanding of how to identify and deal with the effects of pandemics. While we take it for granted that scientists understand viruses, it is important to remember that their study only began in the latter half of the 19th century. Most major discoveries in virology took place after World War II, and breakthroughs continue to be made today. At the turn of the 20th century, when it came to fighting pandemics, we were still very much finding our feet.

② *The Trailing Skirt – Death Loves a Shining Mark*, a satirical cartoon featured in *Puck* magazine, USA, 8 August 1900. The 20th century saw an increasing focus on good hygiene. Detractors believed that trailing skirts – fashionable among turn-of-the-century New Yorkers – were responsible for gathering and spreading germs.

②

Tuberculosis
Neolithic–present

Deadly pandemics do not always arrive with a bang. Because it has afflicted humanity for so long, tuberculosis (TB) has been called the 'slow' pandemic. Thanks to evidence preserved in Neolithic bones and in Egyptian mummies, we know that it has infected humans for at least four millennia, and its destructive path most likely trails much further back into antiquity. Medical advances starting in the late 19th century helped scientists understand TB, and led to prevention and treatment of the disease being developed during the 20th century. But the fight is far from over: since the 1980s, there has been a resurgence in the spread of the illness, and today it claims 1.5 million lives per year – more than any other infectious disease.

TB is an airborne disease, caught through bacteria inhaled from the coughs and sneezes of infected people. The best-known symptom is a persistent and worsening cough, but the disease can also lead to weight loss, fever, tiredness and coughing up blood. While exposure to as few as ten bacteria can cause infection, prolonged and close contact with an infected person is usually required. Today, most healthy people experience no symptoms when infected, with the immune system moving fast to destroy the bacteria. Even if the body fails to quash the bug, only one in ten people will experience immediate symptoms. The disease, instead, becomes latent, lying dormant in the body and causing no ill effects. Those with latent TB who have a normally functioning immune system face a small chance – about ten per cent – that the illness will resurface as active TB at some point in their lives. However, for people with a compromised immune system, such as those living with HIV, the likelihood of latent TB becoming active grows year on year. Indeed, TB kills more HIV-positive people than any other disease.

TB reached epidemic levels across Europe in the 1800s, and it has been estimated that it was responsible for the deaths of at least one in seven people at the time. Great efforts were, therefore, made to find the causes

① A Red Cross worker presents information about TB to a group of people in Saint-Étienne, France, in 1918. ② French children afflicted with TB are looked after by US Red Cross volunteers during World War I. ③ Patients rest in a TB ward in Sainte-Eugénie hospital in Lyon, France. ④ This unknown girl, pictured in hospital in 1917, later died of TB in France.

①

②

③

④

of TB, in order that science might find a way to fight back. The breakthrough came in 1882, when German physician Robert Koch discovered *Mycobacterium tuberculosis*, the bacterium responsible for the spread of the disease, thus proving that TB was contagious. This improved understanding led to the introduction of public health measures, such as sanatoriums for those suffering from the disease and campaigns against spitting.

Treatments up to this point had involved invasive surgical interventions, such as intentionally collapsing a patient's lung. After the discovery of *M. tuberculosis*, the race was on to find a pharmaceutical means of defeating it. However, it was not until 1944 that there was another major breakthrough: the discovery of streptomycin, the first antibiotic that could effectively treat TB. This was followed in the 1950s by isoniazid and in the 1970s by rifampicin, each making the disease easier and quicker to treat.

Alongside public health measures and improved treatments, Koch's discovery led to the development of the Bacillus Calmette–Guérin (BCG) vaccine. Named after its French inventors, Albert Calmette and Camille Guérin, the BCG vaccine was developed in 1908 with a strain of bovine TB taken from the udder of a diseased cow. Seeking to avoid repeating the failures of doomed early attempts to create a TB vaccine, the Lille-based scientists spent 11 years creating subcultures of the bovine cells using glycerine, ox bile and potatoes. The process was repeated 239 times before reaching a level of safety with which they were happy. Calmette and Guérin's vital work was almost halted by the outbreak of World War I, and by the consequent difficulty in obtaining potatoes and ox bile while Lille was under German occupation. After extensive animal testing showed BCG to be safe, human testing of the vaccine started in 1921, and mass production began in 1924. Take-up of the vaccine varied drastically by country, with continental Europe embracing the vaccine, while the United Kingdom and the United States took a more cautious approach. A catastrophe at Lübeck, Germany, in which 73 infants died from TB after receiving the vaccine, also undermined BCG's credibility for some years. The problem was traced to contamination of the vaccine, rather than the formula of the vaccine itself, but significant reputational damage was done.

After World War II, global attention turned again to the spread of TB, and studies confirmed BCG to be safe and effective. Most developed nations, excluding the Netherlands and the United States, began routine inoculation of their populations in the 1950s. At the turn of the 21st century, many developed nations switched to the US approach of targeted testing and contact tracing, and population-wide inoculation programmes were phased out. The developing world still favours mandatory vaccination.

⑤ A World War I poster decries the 'two scourges' to plague France: the Germans and TB. ⑥ Another French poster calls for the defeat of TB, comparing it to the most dangerous reptiles. ⑦ A nurse points to 11 ways to prevent TB in this Italian poster from 1930. ⑧ A Belgian poster from 1937. The Red Cross of Lorraine was chosen as the international symbol of the fight against TB in 1902. ⑨ This Chinese poster calls on people to shun superstitious practices when treating TB in favour of modern medicine.

⑤

⑥

⑦

⑧

⑨

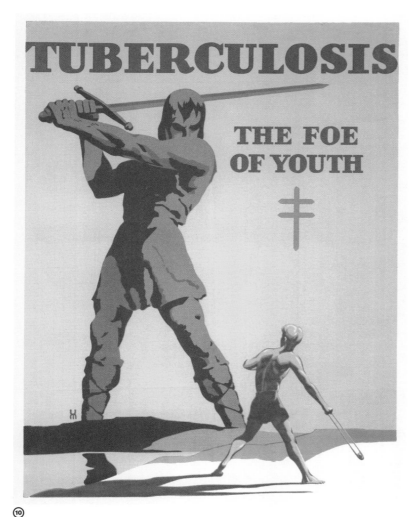

(10)

⑩ This US poster, aimed at young people, depicts a youth as David and TB as Goliath. ⑪ A campaign to encourage people to visit their doctor was paid for by the sale of 'Christmas seals': stamps put on envelopes to raise funds for the fight against TB. ⑫ This US poster features a Christmas seal. These seals were stuck on Christmas card envelopes to raise awareness of TB. ⑬ ⑭ ⑮ These three posters underline the fact that a person can appear healthy while experiencing the early stages of TB. The only way to be sure is to have a diagnostic X-ray of the lungs.

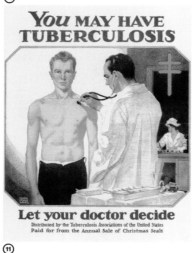

(11)

(12)

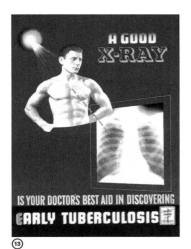

A GOOD X-RAY

IS YOUR DOCTORS BEST AID IN DISCOVERING
EARLY TUBERCULOSIS

(13)

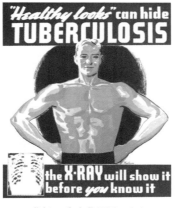

"Healthy looks" can hide
TUBERCULOSIS

the X-RAY will show it
before you know it

Christmas Seals Fight Tuberculosis

(14)

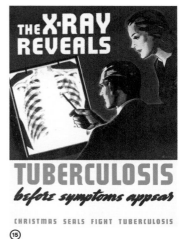

THE X-RAY REVEALS

TUBERCULOSIS
before symptoms appear

CHRISTMAS SEALS FIGHT TUBERCULOSIS

(15)

To determine whether a BCG inoculation is required, a skin test is usually carried out first. Most countries, including the United States and Soviet Union, favoured the Mantoux test, which involves injecting diagnostic 'tuberculin' fluid into the skin. In the United Kingdom, health authorities opted instead for the Heaf test. Administered by firing six spring-loaded needles into the wrist, this test became a feared rite of passage for generations of 13-year-olds until its discontinuation in 2005.

Today, TB is not a concern for most of those living in the developed West, but it remains a serious problem globally. One person is infected every second – it is estimated that a quarter of the world's population is currently infected – and someone dies from TB every 22 seconds. Drug-resistant strains of TB emerged in the 1980s, making the disease far harder to cure. Coupled with the HIV pandemic, this led to a resurgence of the disease, and the World Health Organization declared TB a global health emergency in 1993. Since 2014, the organization has advanced an End TB Strategy to try to halt the pandemic and to reduce incidence of the disease by 80 per cent by 2030. If the strategy is successful, it will finally bring under control a disease that has claimed countless millions of lives over many thousands of years.

Follow these Tips and You Will Live for a Long Time (Suivez ces Conseils Vous Vivrez Longtemps), National Tuberculosis Defence Committee, France, c. 1920

Suivez ces
VOUS VIVREZ

Vivez le plus possible
au grand air

Dormez
la fenêtre ouverte

Tenez-vous droit
à l'école

Prenez un bain
au moins 1 fois par semaine

"Comité National de Défense contre la Tuberculose"
avec le concours de la "Fondation Rockefeller"

During the late 19th and early 20th centuries, scientists gained a better understanding of how illnesses spread. Governments and health authorities began educating the public on how to protect themselves and how to limit the spread of disease to others.

1 Spend as much time as possible outdoors **2** Sleep with the window open **3** Do not put objects in your mouth that may contain other people's saliva **4** Brush your teeth before you go to bed **5** Sit up straight at school **6** Take a bath at least once a week **7** Wash your hands before you sit down to eat **8** Never spit on the ground

Conseils
LONGTEMPS

Ne portez pas à la bouche les objets surlesquels la salive des autres a pu se poser

Brossez-vous les dents avant de vous coucher

Lavez vos mains avant de vous mettre à table

66 bis Rue Notre-Dame-des-Champs _ PARIS. s_ PARIS.
3, Rue de Berri , PARIS.

Ne crachez jamais par terre

_DEVAMBEZ imp. PARIS

'Fighting Tuberculosis' exhibition, National Tuberculosis Association, USA, 1938

TB has afflicted humans for thousands of years, but it took until the late 19th century before the disease began to be fully understood. These charts use simple pictographs, known as 'isotypes', to show how the disease spreads.

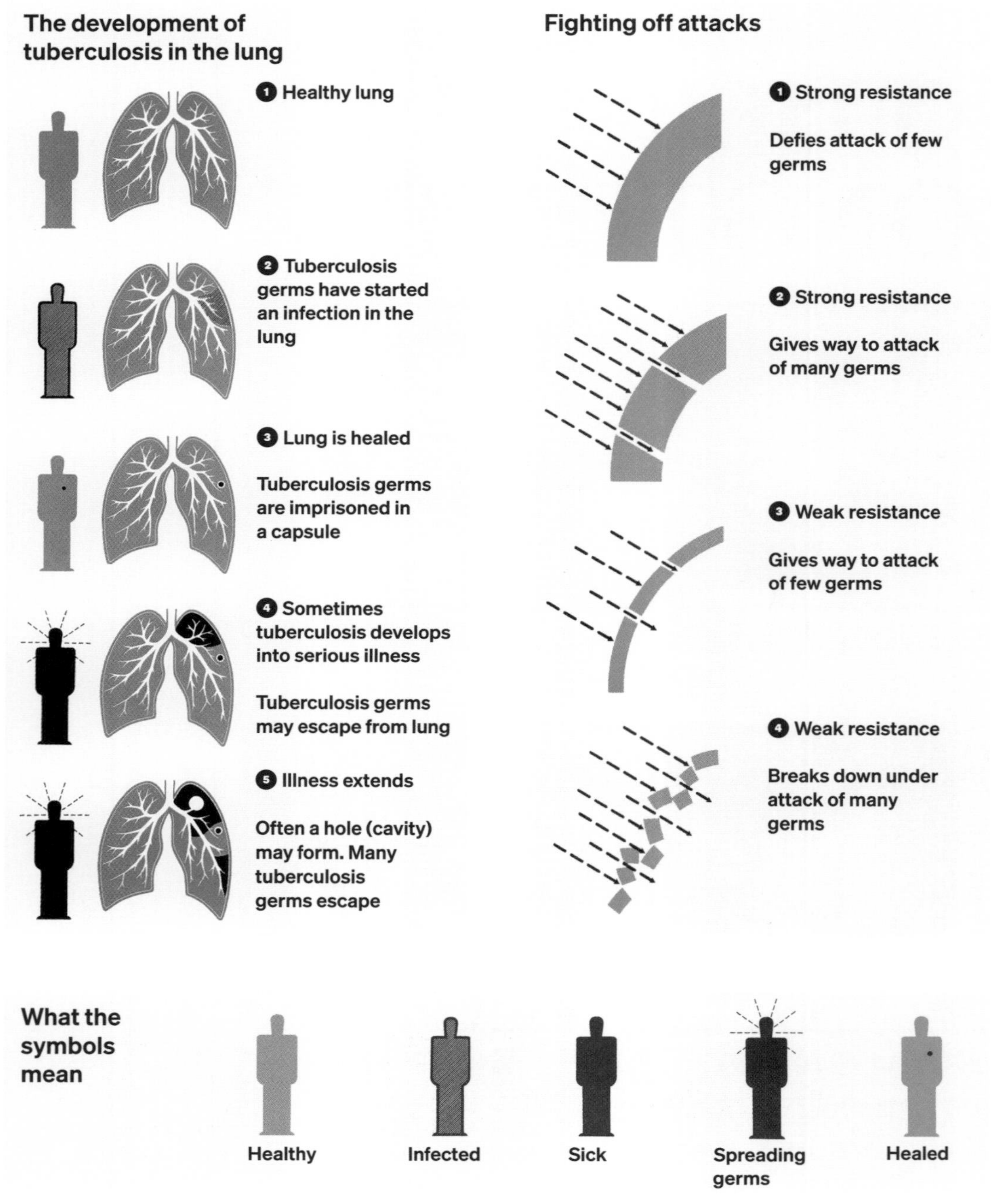

The development of tuberculosis in the lung

1 Healthy lung

2 Tuberculosis germs have started an infection in the lung

3 Lung is healed

Tuberculosis germs are imprisoned in a capsule

4 Sometimes tuberculosis develops into serious illness

Tuberculosis germs may escape from lung

5 Illness extends

Often a hole (cavity) may form. Many tuberculosis germs escape

Fighting off attacks

1 Strong resistance

Defies attack of few germs

2 Strong resistance

Gives way to attack of many germs

3 Weak resistance

Gives way to attack of few germs

4 Weak resistance

Breaks down under attack of many germs

What the symbols mean

Healthy   Infected   Sick   Spreading germs   Healed

Tuberculosis spreads in the household

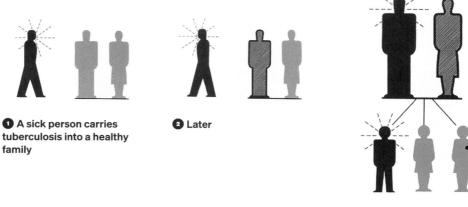

1 A sick person carries tuberculosis into a healthy family

2 Later

3 Still later

Tuberculosis germs are spread from person to person in many ways

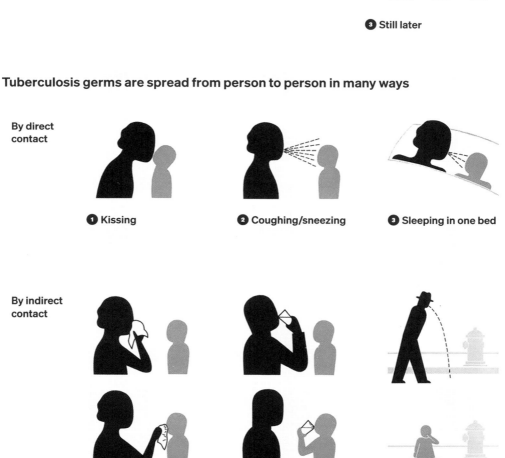

By direct contact

1 Kissing

2 Coughing/sneezing

3 Sleeping in one bed

By indirect contact

1 Common use of personal things

2 Common use of eating utensils

3 Playing where others have spat

Tuberculosis prevention poster campaign, Shanghai Relief Society for the Elderly, China, 1953

Authorities in China encouraged the public to maintain strong physical health and to practise good hygiene to halt the spread of TB. The second poster demonstrates how to dispose of sputum safely.

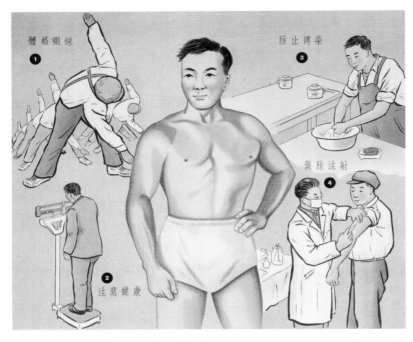

❶ Exercise to stay in good shape ❷ Pay attention to your health ❸ Wash your hands to prevent infections spreading ❹ Get vaccinated

❶ TB patients must not swallow phlegm but spit it into a container and boil it for 20 minutes, before disposing of the contents ❷ Burn tissues ❸ Boil handkerchiefs for 20 minutes, then wash and dry them

These posters show the vast variety of ways in which TB can be transmitted: from talking at close quarters, to sharing utensils and using saliva to count out paper bills.

Overleaf: *To Prevent Tuberculosis*, Publicity Office of the Central Ministry of Health, China, 1953

❶ Means by which TB can be spread through the respiratory system **❷** Coughing **❸** Sneezing **❹** Speaking closely **❺** Feeding, or through mouth to mouth contact **❻** Kissing **❼** Sleeping in a bed together

❶ Means by which TB can be spread through the digestive system **❷** Using saliva to count out money **❸** Sharing meals on the same table as a patient **❹** Using saliva to turn pages **❺** Sharing a handkerchief **❻** Sharing cutlery and crockery

預防肺結核病

怎樣

To prevent tuberculosis

怎樣預防

Ways to avoid catching it

Direct contact with a patient – e.g. coughing, sneezing, speaking – can infect a healthy person

Phlegm should be spat into a container, then emptied into the sewer system

In the workplace, individuals should bring their own cutlery and crockery for meal times

Be conscious to eat a balanced nutritious diet

Establish a healthy routine for sleep, work, study and rest

Ways to spread it

Dried spit on the ground becomes dust and can get blown into the air

A healthy person can be infected by using infected clothing, bedding, cutlery or crockery

Everyone should use a handkerchief to cover their nose and mouth when coughing and sneezing

Get into the habit of washing your hands before meal times

Daily outdoor exercise and sports will strengthen your body and well-being

An annual body check-up will ensure good health and will spot potential signs of early illness, which can then be treated promptly

Tuberculosis prevention poster campaign, Shanghai Relief Society for the Elderly, China, 1953

This series of posters issued by the Chinese authorities uses simple language and illustrations to educate the public about the causes and treatment of TB. It also suggests measures that help prevent the spread of the disease.

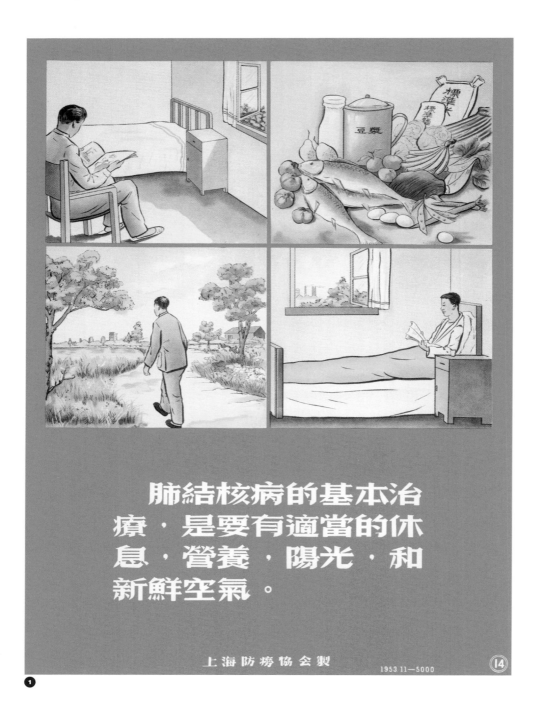

1 The basic treatment for TB is rest, a balanced nutritious diet, sunshine and fresh air **2** The phlegm of a TB patient contains germs. If it is spat onto the ground, it will turn into dust when dry and the germs can spread in the air **3** The early stage of TB is curable. A healthy person should have regular X-ray check-ups to ensure early signs are detected and treated **4** A TB patient should eat separately. Utensils used by the patient should be sterilized and stored separately after each use. Any leftover food needs to boil for 20 minutes before it can be used for any other purposes **5** Any room that has been occupied by a TB patient should be thoroughly and completely sanitized before it is used by another patient

2

肺結核病人的痰中含
有結核桿菌，將痰吐在
地上，乾燥後隨塵埃飛
揚空中，傳染他人。

上海防癆協會製　　1953.11—5000　⑦

3

初起的肺結核病，容易
治好，健康的人，也應該
定期作Ｘ光肺部檢查，達
到「早期發現，早期治療
」的目的。

上海防癆協會製　　1953.11—5000　⑨

4

和肺結核病人一起吃飯，
很容易被傳染，所以要分開
吃，病人的食具用畢消毒後
，也要分開貯藏，病人吃剩
的飯菜，最好煮沸二十分鐘
，然後再加利用。

上海防癆協會製　　1953.11—5000　㉓

5

肺結核病人曾經住
過的房間，必需進行
一次徹底的消毒，才
能再住其他的人。

上海防癆協會製　　1953.11—5000　㉕

Tuberculosis prevention poster campaign, Vellore Christian Medical College, India, 1980s

These posters issued by the Indian public health authorities seek to provide accurate information about TB. As well as explaining its causes and treatment, they encourage people to be vaccinated or to visit the hospital if they experience symptoms of TB.

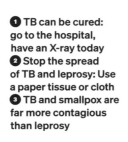

❶ TB can be cured: go to the hospital, have an X-ray today
❷ Stop the spread of TB and leprosy: Use a paper tissue or cloth
❸ TB and smallpox are far more contagious than leprosy

Tuberculosis information boards, National Tuberculosis Institute, India, 1980s

This public health campaign not only provides basic hygiene advice but dispels myths around TB, and encourages people to look out for others.

1 TB can be cured. Drugs cure TB, and all hospitals give the drugs for free. Treatment is for a long period. Follow your doctor's advice. Tonics, a nutritious diet and injections are not always necessary. Bed rest and hospital admission is not always needed
2 Do you know? TB is infectious, not hereditary. TB is caused by small germs. TB germs are in the lungs of TB patients. When they cough, the germs come out and float in the air. When healthy people breathe, the germs get into their lungs. When germs multiply, they damage the lungs and can cause TB
3 Prevent TB...You too can help. Vaccinate your child with BCG. While coughing, cover your mouth. Do not spit everywhere. Persuade TB patients to complete their treatment. Send patients with a cough to hospital

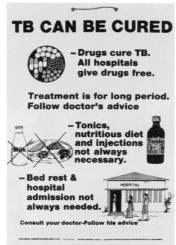

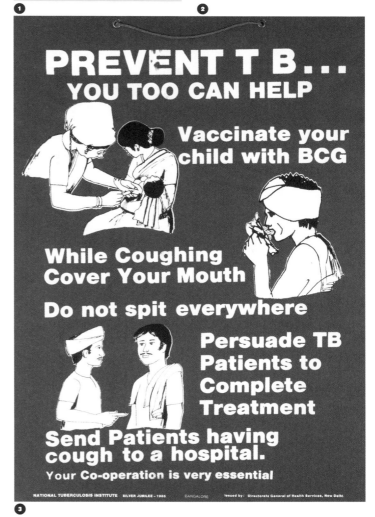

Spanish Flu
1918–20

The first of the 20th-century pandemics, the deadliest and the one that has cast the longest shadow was the Spanish flu. Despite its moniker, it would be fruitless to look to Spain for its origin. Candidates for the disease's real source have included China, India and the battlefields of France, but research suggests it most likely emerged from the heartland of the American Midwest. The flu – more properly, influenza A (H1N1) virus – was first detected at Camp Funston, an army base in rural Kansas. On 4 March 1918, Private Albert Gitchell, who worked in the camp's kitchens, reported symptoms of a fever, sore throat and headache. Before the day was out, hundreds of Gitchell's fellow troops had joined him in the sick bay. In the weeks that followed, the virus – carried by vast movements of troops – began its march across North America and on to Western Europe.

So why was it called the Spanish flu? The epithet was a misnomer driven not so much by nationalism, but by national self-interest. Some governments deliberately withheld information about the flu from the public, leading to events being widely misinterpreted in a way that suggested Spain as the source of the outbreak. With conflict still raging across Europe, the incoming crisis of a pandemic was the last thing warring governments wanted to broadcast. The war's end was by no means in sight, and such news – thought those in power – could deal a potentially devastating blow to national morale. Consequently, they ensured that reporting on the local impact of the virus was kept to a minimum. Neutral countries, on the other hand, were not subject to such press restrictions. In Spain, journalists were free to report on the alarming new virus and generated stacks of news articles; the coverage was further amplified when the Spanish king, Alfonso XIII, suffered a nasty bout of the disease. Combined with radio silence on the pandemic from other countries, these reports gave observers around the world the clear impression that Spain was ground zero for the new virus.

①

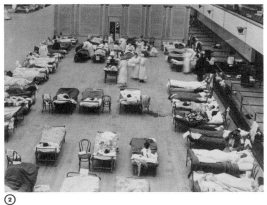

②

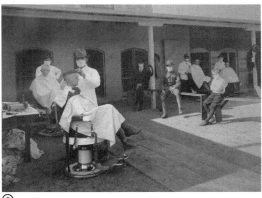

③

① Masks were adopted globally to combat the spread of H1N1, as worn by these Seattle Red Cross workers. ② The 1918 pandemic left health services struggling to cope. Here, Oakland Municipal Auditorium, California, acts as a temporary hospital for patients. ③ In a pandemic, businesses have to adapt to survive. To avoid the Spanish flu, trade moved outdoors at this Berkeley barber shop, 1919.

While early steps to prevent the spread were hampered by government censorship and the ensuing public inaction, the massive movement of troops around the world doubtless exacerbated the problem. It is difficult not to see a meaningful connection between the end of World War I and the surge in cases of Spanish flu. The US army's chief of staff, enabled by President Woodrow Wilson, sought to build US military involvement in the war at any cost, dramatically stepping up the numbers of men being mobilized and sent to Europe. When the US army's surgeon-general pressed the government to prioritize curbing the spread of flu over sending men to fight, he was forced into early retirement. General Erich Ludendorff, the head of the German army, later suggested it had not been the fresh injection of US troops that ended the war, but rather the virus that they brought with them. As the world mourned the 40 million killed in conflict, nobody knew that 50 million more were about to die from the flu.

Cruelly, H1N1 disproportionately targets young adults, meaning those returning war-weary from the front lines were also the most likely to die. Even before the end of the war, it became clear that there was a pressing and immediate need to give precedence to public health and combatting the spread. Officials around the world attempted to provide advice and to change behaviours via public information campaigns.

In October 1918, the French newspaper Le Télégramme des Vosges published advice typical of that being issued by officials around the world, covering what individuals could do to protect themselves from the flu: 'Avoid tiredness, overeating, excesses of all kinds... maintain good hygiene and a substantial diet... give up cold foods and drinks... wash your hands with soapy water... morning and evening, rinse and gargle your mouth with half a glass of boiled water containing a few drops of mint alcohol.' Similar advice on personal hygiene was shared on posters in Italy, where the government primarily sought to reassure the population and maintain order. Here, wartime methods of censorship were adapted to control the flow of information around Spanish flu: any negative findings leaked were immediately put down to rumours spread by internal enemies. Italian officials deliberately chose strong-smelling disinfectant for public spaces in order to convince the public that they were taking action. Indeed, being seen to be doing something – even if it has no discernible effect – is something that crops up time and again when looking at how officials deal with catastrophes.

However, simple personal hygiene was clearly not enough to curb the disease. The way that people interacted in public had to be modified in order to reduce the chance of infecting others. By February 1919, more stringent measures were being put in place to tackle the virus. In Australia, the government of New South Wales made wearing a face covering compulsory. It urgently

④ *Worldwide Diffusion of Influenza: Second Wave*, map in *Bulletin of the History of Medicine*, USA, 1991. Troop movements led to the second wave of the Spanish flu being its deadliest, peaking in the autumn of 1918.

⑤ *Excess Mortality in US Cities During Influenza Pandemic*, USA, 1920. Public health statistics provided a new way to understand pandemics. Excess deaths show the true impact of Spanish flu.

⑥ *Influenza Deaths in US Cities*, USA, 1920. A graph of excess deaths by city offers a window onto how different US municipalities coped with the spread of disease.

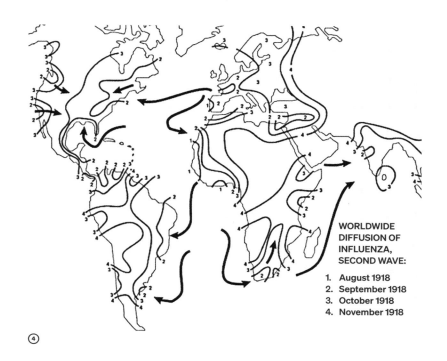

WORLDWIDE DIFFUSION OF INFLUENZA, SECOND WAVE:

1. August 1918
2. September 1918
3. October 1918
4. November 1918

④

EXCESS MORTALITY ɪɴ US·CITIES DURING INFLUENZA EPIDEMIC

PERCENT OF POPULATION DYING

CITY	SEPT. 8 –NOV. 23 10 WEEKS	NOV. 24 –FEB. 1 10 WEEKS	FEB. 2 – MAR 29 8 WEEKS	TOTAL 28 WEEKS
PHILADELPHIA	.69	.01	.03	.73
FALL RIVER	.59	.03	.04	.68
PITTSBURGH	.59	.12	.06	.77
BALTIMORE	.57	.03	.0	.60
SYRACUSE	.55	.02	.02	.58
NASHVILLE	.53	.16	.12	.63
BOSTON	.50	.12	.0	.62
NEW HAVEN	.49	.13	.0	.61
NEW ORLEANS	.49	.21	.0	.71
ALBANY	.48	.03	.02	.53
BUFFALO	.47	.10	.04	.61
WASHINGTON	.45	.12	.0	.59
LOWELL	.44	.10	.03	.56
SAN FRANCISCO	.42	.31	.02	.74
CAMBRIDGE	.39	.12	.0	.50
NEWARK	.36	.11	.04	.53
PROVIDENCE	.36	.13	.03	.55
RICHMOND	.35	.18	.02	.55
DAYTON	.35	.02	.03	.37
OAKLAND	.33	.22	.01	.56
CHICAGO	.30	.09	.04	.46
NEW YORK	.30	.09	.08	.47
CLEVELAND	.27	.11	.04	.42
LOS ANGELES	.26	.26	.01	.55
MEMPHIS	.25	.02	.09	.37
ROCHESTER	.25	.12	.03	.40
KANSAS CITY	.25	.31	.06	.63
DENVER	.24	.36	.07	.63
CINCINNATI	.23	.12	.11	.46
OMAHA	.22	.20	.0	.43
LOUISVILLE	.19	.04	.14	.37
ST. PAUL	.19	.31	.02	.54
COLUMBUS	.19	.15	.07	.41
PORTLAND	.19	.22	.03	.43
TOLEDO	.17	.02	.0	.17
MINNEAPOLIS	.15	.11	.07	.34
SEATTLE	.15	.15	.02	.34
INDIANAPOLIS	.15	.06	.05	.31
BIRMINGHAM	.15	.13	.0	.29
MILWAUKEE	.13	.15	.03	.27
ST. LOUIS	.12	.15	.0	.31
SPOKANE	.11	.15	.03	.22
ATLANTA	.07	.13	.0	.19
GRAND RAPIDS	.04	.15	.04	.19

⑤

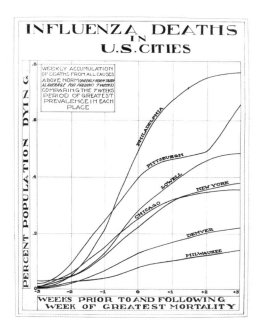

⑥

⑦

⑧

Every Bit Helps—Thank You Editor

METROPOLITAN MOVIES.

⑨

⑦ The use of communal drinking cups was among the behaviours that public health officials sought to change, as shown in this Virginia Health Board flyer from the height of the Spanish flu pandemic. ⑧ *Don't Spit on the Ground!* (*Nicht auf den Boden spucken!*), Germany, 1918. Around the world, authorities ordered the public to stop spitting. They also encouraged people to cover their mouths and noses when coughing or sneezing. ⑨ A boy shows off his giant handkerchief, 'good for a thousand sneezes', in New York City's weekly health department bulletin. ⑩ *Weekly Bulletin of the Department of Health, New York*, USA, 9 November 1918. The cover of this magazine emphasized the importance of covering your nose and mouth when you sneeze. ⑪ *Edmonton Bulletin*, USA, 24 October 1918. This illustration is taken from a feature on making protective masks at home.

ordered 700,000 masks to be made and anyone who refused to wear one could be arrested. In Switzerland, the government initially sought to reassure the public by painting the Spanish flu as a more benign illness than 'war epidemics', such as plague, typhus or cholera. Soon, though, it introduced a raft of preventative measures – a ban on public gatherings, school closures, self-isolation and social distancing – similar to those put in place throughout the COVID-19 pandemic. Chinese posters highlighted the need for face coverings to be worn on public transport and showed how the virus could spread in droplets from coughing passengers.

Posters in the United States targeted common behaviours that were seen to accelerate the spread of disease. 'Careless spitting, coughing and sneezing spread influenza' warned one poster, while New York City's *Weekly Bulletin* chided the public: 'Influenza is spread by the filthy habit of spitting on sidewalks, street cars and other public places. Therefore: Do not spit on the floor or sidewalk.' Another poster was more direct, simply saying: 'Stop spitting – everybody.' Posters with a similar focus on spitting appeared in other countries, including Switzerland.

Putting a stop to public spitting seems like simple common sense today. Other contemporary advice that appeared frequently in messages designed to combat the spread of Spanish flu refers to habits that may be less familiar to the modern reader. In particular, directives to 'shun the common drinking cup' and to stop sharing towels with others featured in materials published by officials in the United States and Poland.

HOW DISEASE IS SPREAD

SNEEZE BUT DONT SCATTER

⑩

How to Make Mask for Prevention of Influenza

⑪

Japan's Central Sanitary Bureau published
this comprehensive manual, titled *Influenza
(流行性感冒)*, in 1918. Colourful illustrations
show how the illness can quickly spread among
ordinary people in day-to-day life, and what
measures can be taken to help prevent infection.

① Coughing without covering your face with your hand is not acceptable. The epidemic cold is transmitted like this! ② Wear a mask on trains and in crowded places. Don't forget to gargle after going out ③ Direct sunshine and doctor's treatments make the plague gods squirm in defeat ④ Protect yourself by separating the living space of parents and children. Space is the enemy of illness ⑤ Remember to wash your hands before meals and to chew food thoroughly

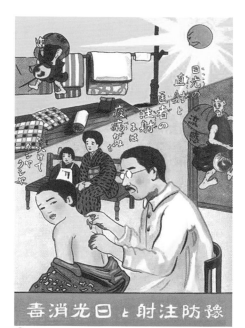

Spanish Influenza, Board of Public Health, Australia, 1918

1 Because the dentist works in the patient's mouth, he must wear a protective mask **2** The subway is a good breeding place for germs, hence ticket sellers must take precautions **3** The barber must be wary of his client's breath and guard against any germs that may lurk in his hair

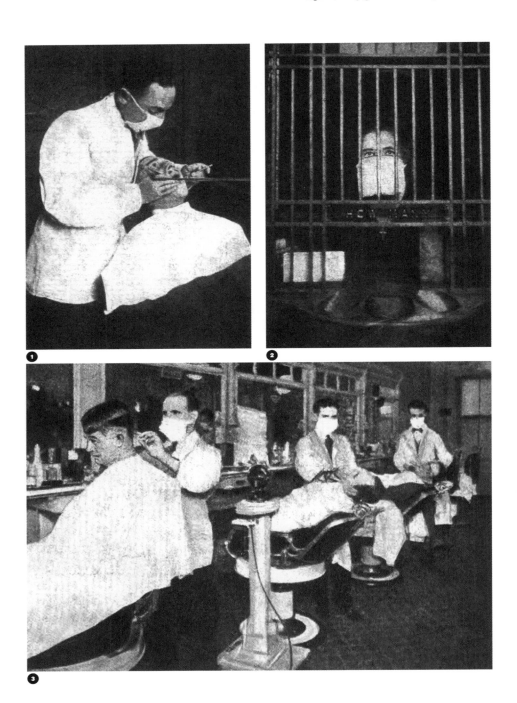

'To Prevent Influenza!', *Illustrated Current News*, USA, 18 October 1918

A US Red Cross nurse covers her nose and mouth with a gauze mask. Such masks were quickly adopted around the world during the Spanish flu pandemic as an effective way of reducing the spread of the deadly disease.

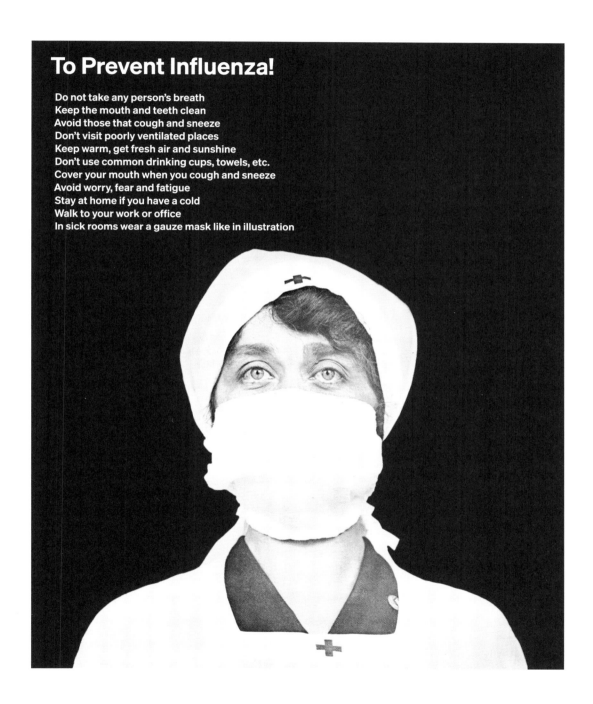

To Prevent Influenza!

Do not take any person's breath
Keep the mouth and teeth clean
Avoid those that cough and sneeze
Don't visit poorly ventilated places
Keep warm, get fresh air and sunshine
Don't use common drinking cups, towels, etc.
Cover your mouth when you cough and sneeze
Avoid worry, fear and fatigue
Stay at home if you have a cold
Walk to your work or office
In sick rooms wear a gauze mask like in illustration

① Japanese children gargle before the school day begins, while awaiting government approval of the Asian flu vaccine, Tokyo, November 1957.
② Despite pandemics being global and uncontrollable by nature, some people seek to apportion blame to particular groups or nations. This billboard appeared in Des Moines, Iowa, 1968.
③ A Chinese student activist wears a mask so he can spread the socialist message without spreading the flu virus. ④ A teacher in Dallas, Texas, gives a lesson to a drastically reduced number of students during the Asian flu pandemic.

HONG KONG FLU IS UNAMERICAN !
Catch Something Made in the U.S.A.

Asian Flu, 1957
Hong Kong Flu, 1968

Despite the enormity of its global impact, the Spanish flu has remained something of a footnote to World War I in our collective consciousness. Its centenary may have gone some way to cementing its place in modern history, particularly since the COVID-19 pandemic came hot on its heels. However, the two flu pandemics that took place in the mid-20th century seem to have made even less of an impression on our shared story. While they proved less deadly than the Spanish flu, the disinterested approach of governments around the world to mitigating these pandemics now seems at best careless and at worst negligent.

First appearing in China early in 1957, Asian flu (H2N2) took full advantage of the Jet Age. As international travel became more common, H2N2 acted as a deadly stowaway, quietly making its way around the world by road, rail and air. By April 1957, a quarter of a million cases had emerged in Hong Kong, and by early summer, one million were infected in India. By late summer, the exceptionally infectious virus had spread to Europe and the United States.

Unlike its predecessor, Asian flu targeted the young and old alike. It acted quickly, with many patients dying within days of falling sick. Despite a clear crisis emerging, however, many of the measures we now associate with pandemics – global alerts, social distancing, mass testing, enforced face coverings and the race to develop a vaccine – did not materialize.

China, which was not a member of the World Health Organization, chose not to inform other countries of the outbreak. Indeed, it was not until the virus made its way to Singapore that the alarm was raised. Western governments were not at pains to respond, nor did they seem to be overly worried about the human impact of the disease. In the United Kingdom, daily life and public events went ahead as usual, despite the risk. Prime Minister Harold Macmillan and his government appear to have been more concerned about bad press, and declined to warn the public in a substantive way. Rather than coordinating a national response, the Ministry of Health advised local medical officers to make their own plans. Better remembered than the pandemic is the United Kingdom's worst nuclear accident: the fire at Windscale nuclear reactor. It took place in October 1957, and response to the incident was hampered by reactor staff being off work sick with Asian flu.

In the United States, the Eisenhower administration refused, on ideological grounds, to create a public vaccination programme and expected the private sector to take care of the nation's needs. It also failed to restrict public gatherings. Consequently, when Asian flu arrived on US shores, it travelled with ease across the country as people continued to move freely, attending conferences and summer camps. Fortunately, US biologist Maurice Hilleman had been monitoring the outbreak from the beginning, and his team's vaccine – created despite the federal government's foot dragging – was deployed just as H2N2 began to affect the United States. Hilleman is now credited with severely reducing the impact of the pandemic.

All this is reflected in the type and volume of information available to the public about Asian flu: official guidance was far less evident than it had been during the Spanish flu. Advertisers took advantage of public fears, filling the void left by health officials to push common cold remedies, which, of course, would have been ineffective against the virus.

In total, the Asian flu pandemic killed 20,000 in the United Kingdom, 80,000 in the United States and some two million worldwide. But it is important to note that it did not simply go away: transmission continued for the next decade, and it became a seasonal virus with a deadly resurgence each winter. This pattern continued until 1968, when the virus mutated into, and was quickly replaced by, a new variant: Hong Kong flu (H3N2). Again, and perhaps because pandemic flu had been an annual visitor for more than a decade, official guidance on the new virus was scant. As with Asian flu, Hong Kong flu remained a background presence in everyday life. For example, during the 1969 recording sessions for the Beatles' album *Let It Be*, Paul McCartney jokingly blamed his lacklustre vocals on the virus.

A vaccine was created by the same team that had countered the Asian flu, but it came after the peak of infection in most countries. Ultimately, Hong Kong flu was responsible for the deaths of 30,000 people in the United Kingdom, 100,000 in the United States and between one and four million worldwide. Following a second wave in the winter of 1969, it retreated to become a seasonal flu.

⑤

⑤ A typist in Manchester, UK, wears a shop-bought mask, intended to prevent being infected with the Asian flu.
⑥ A makeshift Asian flu ward houses 850 sailors, including the entire crew of HMS *Ganges*, in Ipswich, UK. ⑦ In the United States, hens' eggs are infected with the Asian flu virus, a key stage in producing a vaccine.

⑥

⑦

Advertisements for remedies for Asian flu, USA, 1957–58

The slow official response to the Asian flu pandemic was an opportunity for quick-thinking drug companies. Advertisements for cold remedies could be amended to claim efficacy against symptoms of the virus. But the only real remedy was the vaccine.

①

②

③

④

① Advertisement for Musterole medicinal rub, 1957. ② Advertisement for Mistol Mist nasal spray, 1958.

③ Advertisement for St Joseph aspirin, 1958. ④ Advertisement for St Joseph aspirin for children, 1958.

Asian flu television advert, Communicable Disease Centre, USA, 1957

With the advent of the Asian flu vaccine, television campaigns encouraged Americans to get themselves – and their families – immunized: 'Once the disease strikes your community, it is too late.'

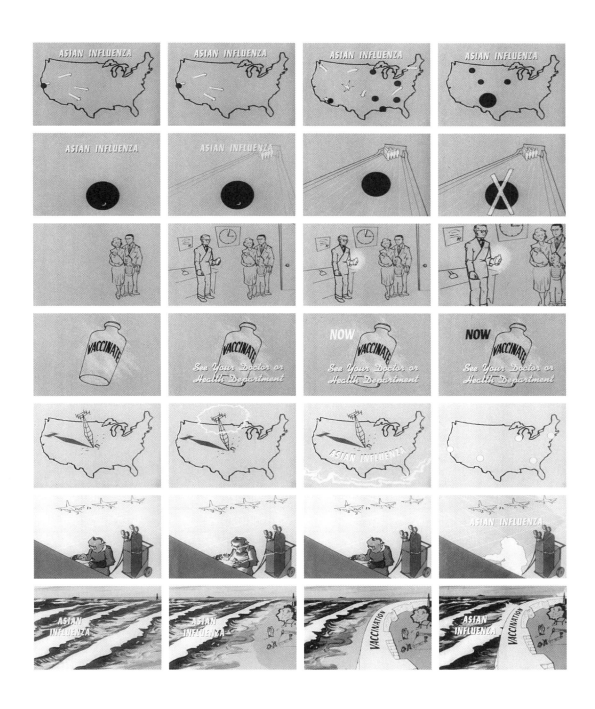

HIV/AIDS
1981–present

In the 1980s, AIDS, and the human immunodeficiency viruses (HIV) that cause it, presented a new and unexpected challenge to governments and health authorities. Retrospective testing of blood samples from the 1950s has shown that HIV has certainly infected humans since 1959; by the 1970s it was silently circulating around the world. In 1981, doctors in the US raised the alarm after noticing patterns of gay men contracting unusual diseases, such as a rare form of skin cancer. After AIDS was first clinically observed, but before its causes were properly understood, the press termed it 'GRID' – gay-related immune deficiency. The view that the disease was somehow intrinsically linked with homosexuality was frequently reflected in the media. In the United Kingdom, for example, reporters freely used terms such as the 'gay plague'. In the US, links were drawn in the popular imagination between those suffering from the illness and groups on the margins of society, particularly gay communities and intravenous drug users. Some

even referred disparagingly to the '4-H Club' of homosexuals, haemophiliacs, heroin users and Haitians.

The disease was named AIDS in 1982, and scientists clinically isolated the underlying HIV virus the following year. However, there was little public interest in AIDS or political will to deal with it; researchers despaired at scant government funding, while those living with AIDS suffered tremendous ill-treatment. It would be a further two years before President Reagan spoke publicly about the illness, in 1985. By then, it was already too late. It is now widely accepted that the association between HIV and marginalized communities significantly delayed any serious political or public health response. The same faulty association also gave people outside of those marginalized groups a false sense of safety, further contributing to the pandemic spread of the virus.

As it became clear to the medical community that the media portrayal of the disease was inaccurate, there was a pressing need for universal

① Members of a mutual help group for people with AIDS approach a lagoon in Chilca, Peru, November 1996. The black lake mud at Chilca is said to have therapeutic properties. ② A fireman, equipped to deal with hazardous materials, removes bags of HIV-infected blood from a truck in Sydney, Australia, May 1990. The improperly transported bags were leaking onto a residential street. ③ Gay rights activists dressed as Death during a rally in San Francisco. In January 1985, this photograph accompanied a feature in the *San Francisco Chronicle* by Randy Shilts, titled '1984 The Year of the Plague'. ④ An AIDS patient is treated at Bichat–Claude Bernard Hospital in Paris, 1992.

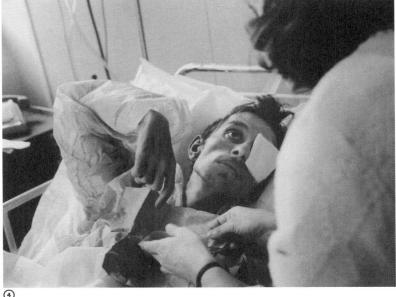

(5)

(6)

(7)

(8)

1. Pandemic

campaigns to educate the public. The UK government was the first to invest in a nationwide publicity drive in 1986, warning of the danger posed to everybody by HIV/AIDS. Still remembered for its shockingly bleak imagery, the campaign and its slogan – 'Don't Die of Ignorance' – reflected the government's view that there was a real risk that AIDS could lead to millions of deaths.

Other countries were slower to react. The World Health Organization's Special Programme on AIDS began in 1987. In the same year, the US federal government launched its 'America Responds to AIDS' campaign. It was aimed at a universal audience, but this was not simply because AIDS was a universal threat: the Reagan administration had created legislation that explicitly banned advertisements that promoted or encouraged homosexual activities. Like the UK publicity, the US campaign relied heavily on creating fear of AIDS, eschewing subtlety in favour of stark imagery such as skeletons and gravestones. One curious poster aimed at Native Americans tied the message to a deeper cultural heritage, depicting AIDS as an owl, and explaining: 'The owl represents prophecy, and is also an omen of prolonged illness and death.'

As campaigns progressed into the 1990s, the imagery became less dramatic and began to be replaced by more traditional public health messages. Reading between the lines, though, we can see that officials still faced a battle to convince the public that the risk was not limited to same-sex liaisons.

The West has not held the monopoly on misinformation around AIDS and the politicization of public health responses to the crisis. In the first decade of the 21st century, South African president Thabo Mbeki pursued policies supportive of AIDS denialism, replacing anti-HIV drugs with herbal remedies and denying government funding to breakthrough clinical treatments. These policies are believed to have led to the deaths of an estimated 365,000 people.

Recent advances in pharmaceutical treatment of HIV mean that many of those living with the virus in the developed world can lead normal lives. Areas such as sub-Saharan Africa, however, remain in the grip of the pandemic, and campaigns to educate the public about AIDS therefore continue around the world.

⑤ *Bleachman*, San Francisco AIDS Foundation, USA, 1988. This poster uses the character of Bleachman to encourage drug users to sterilize their needles. ⑥ *Care Enough to Love Safely*, AIDS Counselling Trust, Zimbabwe, 1991. This Zimbabwean advertisement encourages safe sex while emphasizing family and patriotism. ⑦ *Condoman*, Department of Health, Housing and Community Services, Australia, 1990. The indigenous Australian superhero Condoman was used to promote the idea that it is manly to practise safe sex. ⑧ *Talk to Us*, Keith Haring, USA, 1989. This poster, issued by the New York Department of Health, advertises a hotline offering counselling and medical referrals.

Living Positively with HIV and AIDS, Committed Communities Development Trust, India, 1997

Health officials in Mumbai issued a series of posters tackling the HIV/AIDS pandemic. The first known case of HIV was diagnosed in India in 1986; in 1992, the National AIDS Control Organization was founded to oversee prevention and control strategies. Today, 2.1 million people live with HIV in India – the third largest HIV epidemic in the world.

① Get medical help whenever you feel unwell **②** Eat nutritious food **③** Keep active and busy **④** Take plenty of rest **⑤** Practise good hygiene **⑥** Avoid heavy smoking and do not drink alcohol **⑦** Use condoms **⑧** It is advisable not to get pregnant

Opposite, activities that do not pose a risk for contracting HIV

① Living with your family **②** Swimming together **③** Sharing clothes **④** Being bitten by mosquitos or other insects **⑤** Working together **⑥** Coughing or sneezing **⑦** Travelling on busy transportation **⑧** Playing sports together

Inset illustrations from HIV/AIDS information poster, UNICEF, India, 1997

Poor understanding of the risks posed by the virus meant that people living with HIV/AIDS were severely stigmatized. Part of the duty of public health campaigns was to allay those fears. In contrast to posters depicting the human suffering caused by the disease, these images show that those living with the virus do not present a public health risk in everyday situations.

Recent Viruses
2009–present

Globalization, population growth and cheap travel show no signs of slowing in the 21st century, and recent pandemics demonstrate that viruses continue to take advantage of this situation. In an age driven by instant communication via the Internet, social media and rolling television news, governments have had to adapt how they communicate risk. However, traditional responses to pandemics remain an important part of the communications arsenal available to health officials.

In 2009, a new strain of influenza A (H1N1) – the same virus that caused the Spanish flu – emerged in Mexico, and its spread led to the declaration of a pandemic by the World Health Organization. While this pandemic – Swine flu – is now thought to have infected more people than the Spanish flu, it resulted in far fewer deaths – below a quarter of a million – because this strain was only about as dangerous as seasonal flu. The response of governments, therefore, ended up being muted. Travellers were advised to hold off on making nonessential journeys, while some countries, including China, Egypt, Russia and Taiwan, briefly introduced quarantine measures. In the United Kingdom, a website was launched that allowed people to self-diagnose and request medication. In the United States, the press shared photographs of President Barack Obama receiving an H1N1 vaccination.

An outbreak of a new coronavirus that caused severe acute respiratory syndrome, known as SARS-CoV-1, occurred between 2002 and 2004. While SARS was not a pandemic – around 800 deaths were attributed to the disease, mostly in Asia – it did cause worldwide concern. In China, where the disease started and where most cases occurred, the law was updated to deal with future outbreaks, and a public information campaign was created to explain the changes. In Hong Kong, SARS was depicted as a public hygiene problem, attributed to poor food handling practices, dirty restaurant toilets and too much spitting. This led to a taskforce called Team Clean being set up to make the city 'truly clean and hygienic'. In Singapore, the government's paternalistic attitude was reflected in its response to SARS: it invoked military-style language to portray the disease as a deadly enemy that posed a threat to national integrity, using notions such as 'sacrifice' to

① Medics from the Russian military assist Italian doctors during the first months of the COVID-19 pandemic, 2020. ② A worker in full personal protective equipment sanitizes a Mumbai street in May 2021, when India was recording more than 4,500 COVID-19 deaths every day. ③ People form a socially distanced queue outside a COVID-19 vaccination centre in Delhi, India, in early 2021. ④ A scientist in Rome works to develop a vaccine for COVID-19. Inoculation programmes began in late 2020.

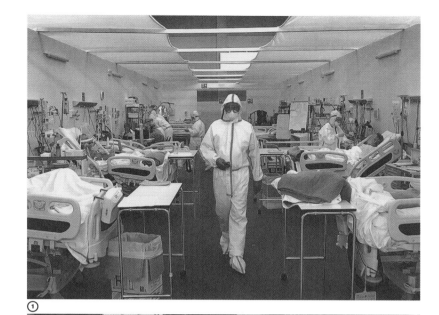

①

②

③

④

encourage people to change their behaviours and help curb the spread. Kits containing 'Fever-Free' stickers were handed out, and these briefly became, according to *The Straits Times*, 'the new national must-have accessory'.

Scientists had been warning of the inevitability of another pandemic for many years, and some organizations were beginning to take those warnings seriously. In 2013, a report by the World Bank called the risk higher than the risk from terrorism, stating that it would bring 'shared misery, economic decline and societal disruptions on a global scale'. It was just one of the organizations recommending an early warning system to detect and quickly control the spread of a future pandemic. Furthermore, as the report pointed out, the cost of such a system would be 'not only modest, but also ten times less than the cost of inaction'. However, action was not taken soon enough.

SARS-CoV-1 may not have escalated to become a pandemic, but its sibling, SARS-CoV-2, did. The virus caused the COVID-19 outbreak, which was first identified in December 2019. A public health emergency was declared in January 2020, and it was officially named a pandemic in March 2020. COVID-19 has caused millions of deaths and immense disruption to societies in every country around the world. The response of governments has been to introduce a level of official guidance not seen since the Spanish flu, alongside new types of public information tailored to our technologically connected world.

The threat from pandemic disease continues. While they have not yet led to a pandemic, two subtypes of Avian flu – H5N1 and H7N9 – have been raising concerns among health officials since the turn of the millennium. Both caused epidemics with high mortality rates – up to 60 per cent – in those who became infected, but both retreated before reaching pandemic levels. Another threat lies in other novel coronaviruses, such as MERS – Middle East respiratory syndrome – which has claimed 858 victims to date since it was identified in 2012. As long as humanity exists, it seems that we will be engaged in a perpetual battle against pandemic diseases. As the global population increases, and the world grows ever closer, the threat will only intensify.

It benefits us all to be prepared.

Modern coronaviruses and influenzas

Data taken from WHO

Avian flu

First identified infection 1997

Virus	Influenza A, H5N1
Strain	HPAI A(H5N1)
Pandemic	No
Territories	18
Deaths	456 (2003–21)
Fatality	c. 56%

SARS

First identified infection 2002

Virus	Coronavirus
Strain	SARS-CoV–1
Pandemic	November 2002–July 2003
Territories	29+
Deaths	774 (2002–03)
Fatality	c. 9.6%

Swine flu

First identified infection 2009

Virus	Influenza A, H1N1
Strain	A/H1N1pdm09
Pandemic	June 2009–August 2010
Territories	214+
Deaths	18,449 (2009–10)
Fatality	c. 0.01%

MERS

First infection identified 2012

Virus	Coronavirus
Strain	MERS-CoV
Pandemic	No
Territories	27
Deaths	888 (2012–21)
Fatality	c. 35%

COVID-19

First infection identified 2019

Virus	Coronavirus
Strain	SARS-CoV-2
Pandemic	March 2020–present
Territories	Worldwide
Deaths	5 million+ (2020–present)
Fatality	As yet unknown

Catch It, Bin it, Kill it, National Health Service, UK, 2009

The Swine flu outbreak in 2009 was classified as just one step below a full-blown pandemic by the World Health Organization. When five people in the United Kingdom tested positive for the virus, the government quickly launched this campaign to encourage good public hygiene.

❶ Catch It: Germs spread easily. Always carry tissues and use them to catch your cough or sneeze ❷ Bin It: Germs can live for several hours on tissues. Dispose of your tissue as soon as possible ❸ Kill it: Hands can transfer germs to every surface you touch. Clean your hands as soon as you can

CATCH IT

Germs spread easily. Always carry tissues and use them to catch your cough or sneeze.

BIN IT

Germs can live for several hours on tissues. Dispose of your tissue as soon as possible.

KILL IT

Hands can transfer germs to every surface you touch. Clean your hands as soon as you can.

MERS-CoV: Preventative Messages for Hajj and Umrah Pilgrims, World Health Organization, worldwide, 2017

A key date in the Islamic calendar, the Hajj sees millions of pilgrims from around the world descend on Mecca to perform their religious duty. Unfortunately, this also helps to create ideal conditions for diseases such as the MERS coronavirus to spread.

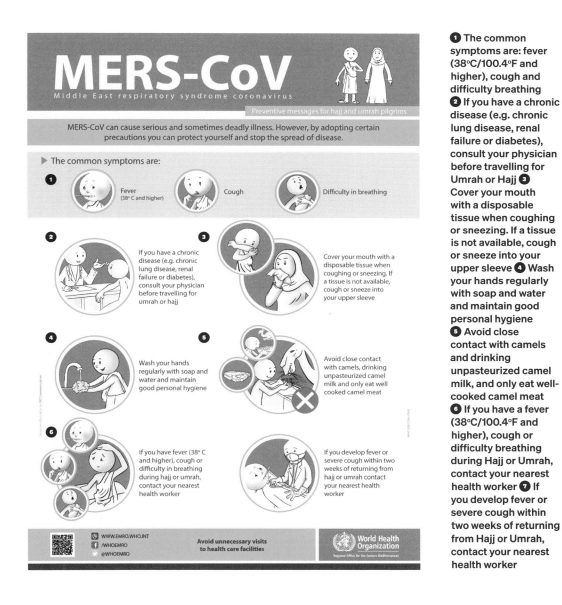

❶ The common symptoms are: fever (38°C/100.4°F and higher), cough and difficulty breathing ❷ If you have a chronic disease (e.g. chronic lung disease, renal failure or diabetes), consult your physician before travelling for Umrah or Hajj ❸ Cover your mouth with a disposable tissue when coughing or sneezing. If a tissue is not available, cough or sneeze into your upper sleeve ❹ Wash your hands regularly with soap and water and maintain good personal hygiene ❺ Avoid close contact with camels and drinking unpasteurized camel milk, and only eat well-cooked camel meat ❻ If you have a fever (38°C/100.4°F and higher), cough or difficulty breathing during Hajj or Umrah, contact your nearest health worker ❼ If you develop fever or severe cough within two weeks of returning from Hajj or Umrah, contact your nearest health worker

Alcohol handrub hand hygiene technique – for visibly clean hands, National Health Service, UK, 2020

Early in the COVID-19 pandemic, health authorities moved to instil basic hygiene practices among the general public. This UK poster shows the complex series of manoeuvres required to ensure the hands are completely clean.

Alcohol handrub hand hygiene technique – for visibly clean hands

1 Apply a small amount (about 3 ml/0.1 fl oz) of the product in a cupped hand

2 Rub the hands together palm to palm, spreading the handrub over the hands

3 Rub the back of each hand with the palm of the other hand with the fingers interlaced

4 Rub palms with fingers interlaced

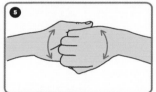

5 Rub the back of the fingers to the opposing palms with fingers interlocked

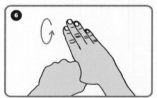

6 Rub each thumb clasped in the opposite hand using a rotational movement

7 Rub the tips of the fingers in the opposite palm in a circular motion

8 Rub each wrist with the opposite hand

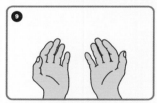

9 Wait until the product has evaporated and the hands are dry (do not use paper towels)

10 The process should take 15–30 seconds

cleanyourhands® campaign

National Patient Safety Agency

Stay Safe/Stay Sane online poster platform, worldwide, 2020–21

In an increasingly interconnected world, people can come together to create a truly global response to events that affect us all. This project invited artists to share their own take on public information posters during the COVID-19 pandemic.

❶ Get the Fuck Inside/Covid-19 Kills ❷ Stay Home/Break the Chain ❸ Try Your Best Not to Stress ❹ Pyjamas are the New Bahamas ❺ Rediscover your Balcony ❻ Staying Home is Staying Safe ❼ Do You Greet, or Corona? (a common saying in Egypt during the pandemic) ❽ Stay Social/Stay Distant ❾ Don't Forget to Wrap Them Up ❿ Keep Them Filthy Bastards Clean ⓫ Stay at Home/Protect Yourself ⓬ How to Wear a Face Mask Properly

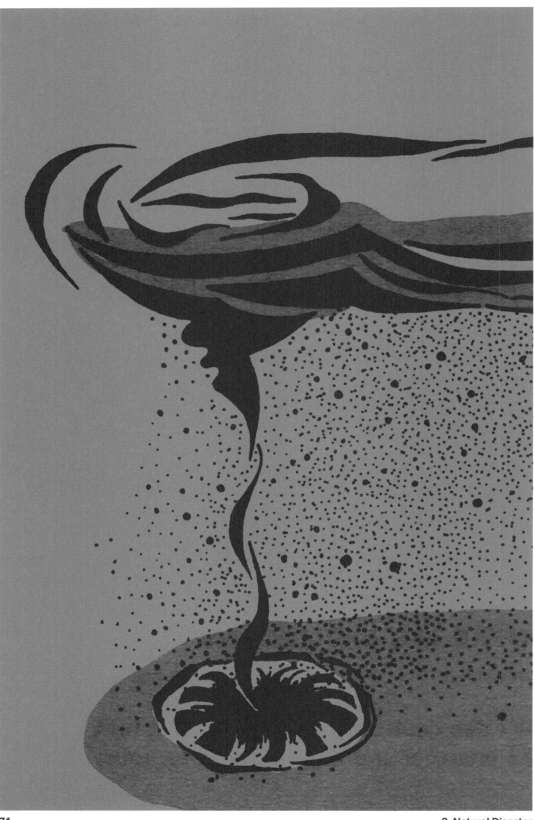

Natural Disaster

Extreme Weather   82
When the Earth Moves   102
Fighting Fire   126
Survive in the Wild   140

①

In Time of Emergency*

Preparing for Natural Disasters

① Uncle Sam, the personification of the US government, warns Americans to be vigilant against forest fires in this poster issued in the 1930s.

Natural disasters such as earthquakes, volcanic eruptions and extreme weather events can strike at any time, often occurring swiftly and with little warning. This makes them difficult to prepare for. In areas where natural disasters are more likely to occur, survival can only be ensured by embedding emergency preparedness education into the fabric of daily life. Short-term public information campaigns do not suffice.

Modern meteorologists can provide authorities with some advance notice of extreme weather events, such as tornados or flash floods. A short but critical period of warning allows governments to issue safety guidance and the public to take steps to protect themselves, such as shoring up or evacuating their homes. Advance warning of geological events is far trickier. Although scientists can now, under the right conditions, predict volcanic activity with some confidence, nobody – according to the US Geological Survey – has yet succeeded in predicting a major earthquake. The one 'known' when it comes to natural disasters is physical geography. We have some idea of areas where the risk is higher, such as in tornado zones, along geological fault lines, near active volcanoes or on flood plains.

In addition to the unpredictable nature of natural disasters, those tasked with protecting the public must now also contend with the exacerbating effects of man-made climate change. These are already being seen, including shrinking glaciers and the loss of sea ice, longer and hotter heatwaves and the melting of permafrost. It is less clear, at present, what effect these changes will have in terms of geological natural disasters; however, there is growing evidence that severe storms and flooding affect the Earth's crust and can be directly linked to increased geological activity such as earthquakes and even volcanic eruptions.

In mild, temperate areas, where extreme weather is rare, there is some evidence that climate change is leading to changing weather patterns. This means fewer cold winters and more extremes of wet and windy weather, such as flooding and hurricanes. The United States has seen tragedies like Hurricane Katrina in 2005, which resulted in more than 1,800 deaths and around $161 billion of damage. NASA scientists have suggested that North Atlantic hurricanes will continue to increase in intensity, frequency and duration. In places

② This map charts the paths of the worst hurricanes to hit the United States' east coast between 1900 and 1944.

2. Natural Disaster

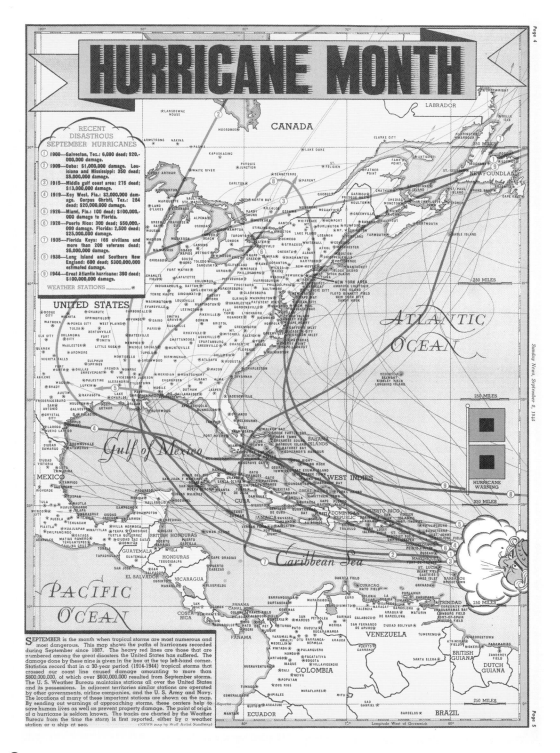

③

④

⑤

⑥

Extinction Rebellion emerged in the late 2010s as a new global environmental protest movement. Its approach of nonviolent direct action and civil disobedience is reflected in the bold imagery and anarchic graphic design choices of its campaign materials. The stylized hourglass symbol represents 'time running out' for the world to face up to climate change and ecological collapse.

already affected by heatwaves, increasing temperatures are predicted to cause more prolonged droughts. In Southeast Asia, monsoon seasons have already been seen to be behaving erratically, with some years experiencing earlier monsoons and more rainfall than expected.

Climate change is truly a global problem. The melting of Arctic sea ice leads directly to rising sea levels, impacting coastal communities around the world. Greenland lost a record 586 billion tonnes (532 billion tons) of ice in 2019, and that loss appears to be accelerating. In the same year, unprecedented numbers of wildfires hit parts of North and South America, Southeast Asia and Australia. Africa's Sahel zone, a belt of semi-arid land across the continent, has been hit by increasingly intense droughts, leading to the devastation of agriculture, while parts of Indonesia are gradually being flooded. Mass migration caused by climate change has already started; it is feared that, in the coming decades, displaced populations will be counted not in the millions, but in the billions.

The effects of climate change are already making it more difficult to keep the public informed and ready to cope when the environment strikes back. Governments must now make substantial investments in preparing for natural disasters to ensure lives can continue to be saved.

Extreme Weather

Extreme weather can be classed as a natural disaster when it arrives suddenly, with little or no warning, and is of sufficient intensity to cause loss of life. The threat from extreme weather is usually determined by the physical features of a region, meaning certain parts of the world are more at risk than others. For example, a wide north-to-south strip of the central United States known as 'Tornado Alley' hosts the majority of the country's 1,000 tornados each year. Tornado Alley is the result of two weather fronts colliding: cold, dry air blown from the north-west, and warm, moist air from the Gulf of Mexico in the south-east. Where the fronts combine, deadly rotating winds with speeds up to 512 km/h (318 mph) are generated. At their most destructive, tornados can carry heavy objects for several kilometres, uproot forests and lift houses off their foundations – destroying entire towns and killing hundreds each year. Consequently, it is vital that warning systems are in place to give the public as much notice as possible.

Tornado warnings are broadcast when a tornado has been spotted – either in person or on weather radar – trying to form or land. A warning is distinct from a 'tornado watch', which is simply a notice that the conditions are right for a twister to form. Since the broadcast of the first tornado alert in 1948, areas where tornados are likely to form have created and refined complex systems for contacting people. The lead time for tornado warnings has improved dramatically throughout the 20th century, thanks to advancements in radar forecasting technology and established reporting systems for the public. Yet, even with such progress, the average warning time is still only around 15 minutes, and some 70 per cent of warnings prove to be false alarms.

Where tornados are common, governments must, therefore, make sure that the public knows what to look for and how to act when they see one. Programmes of tornado preparedness have been in place since the 1950s to ensure people are aware of the warning signs: dark, greenish, rotating

① The dark funnel of a tornado looms ominously over Oklahoma, 1898. ② Chickens run free after their hut is destroyed by a hurricane in Massachusetts, 1938. ③ A man grabs a young tree to steady himself during a hurricane in Brooklyn, New York, 1954. ④ A corpse is carried away from wreckage caused by a disastrous hurricane and flood in Galveston, Texas, 1900. ⑤ Local people pose on a house ripped from its foundations by storm weather in New Jersey, c. 1900.

①

②

③

④

⑤

⑥ The working class district of Honjo, Tokyo, copes with a flood in the early 20th century.
⑦ Venetians navigate St Mark's Square by boat in 1953, during the city's worst flood for half a century.
⑧ A neighbourhood flooded by the Los Angeles River in December 1951.
⑨ A double-decker bus in Hartlepool, UK, braves a 20-m (65-ft) stretch of floodwater, 1963.

⑥

⑦

⑧

⑨

clouds, large hailstones appearing without rain and a roaring wind, often compared to the sound of a freight train. Public awareness of the tell-tale signs of an impending tornado also helps to bolster the tornado reporting system. During so-called 'outbreaks' of tornados, authorities are heavily reliant on the public calling in sightings, and US regional television stations will cancel their scheduled programmes in order to have an open channel to issue live reports.

However, the United States is not the only place to experience tornados; indeed, they have been seen on every continent except Antarctica. Areas of Germany, Italy and France have been labelled Europe's 'tornado alleys'; in reality, though, tornados happen across much of the continent. Surprisingly, the United Kingdom has more tornados per square kilometre than anywhere else on the planet. It was here that the largest registered European outbreak took place in 1981, when more than 100 tornados – albeit weak ones – were seen in a single day. At the time, this made it the second largest outbreak in recorded history.

The lack of public preparedness in places where the phenomenon is less common has resulted in numerous injuries and occasional fatalities, including 36 deaths when a tornado hit Venice and Padua, Italy, in 1970, and as many as 400 deaths during a spate of tornados that hit the Soviet Union in 1984.

Severe flooding is another type of extreme weather that occurs frequently in certain parts of the world. It is a particular challenge in Southeast Asia, which has an annual monsoon season. While floods can be anticipated and prepared for up to a point, thousands of lives are still lost each year in unexpected flash floods and landslides caused by torrential rain. Flood warning systems in these places are well-established, and work to refine them is ongoing. But, as with any disaster preparedness, the human factor is at least as important as the technological one. Authorities worldwide continue to conduct studies in order to better understand how flood alerts are interpreted, whether they are believed and how they are acted on by ordinary people. By taking this research into account, flood warnings and public information campaigns can be improved and lives can be saved.

As with other forms of extreme weather, flooding is more likely to be catastrophic if it occurs in a place where it has not happened in recent times. For much of the 20th century, London, which lies on the River Thames, was under persistent threat of severe flooding between September and April each year. Before adequate defences were built, local authorities had to continuously run public information campaigns to remind Londoners of the threat. It was imperative that the city's population knew how they should act should a flood warning be broadcast, and anyone living or working in London was encouraged to learn their Thames Flood Drill. This continued until the Thames Barrier was completed in 1982.

In Time of Emergency, Office of Civil Defence, USA, 1968

Distributed via the United States' network of community civil defence services, this manual contains advice on surviving natural disasters, including floods, earthquakes, tornados and extreme winter weather. It describes the signals

Advice for flooding

1 Travel with care:
Leave early enough so as not to be marooned by flooded roads, fallen trees and wires. Make sure you have enough fuel in your car.
Follow recommended routes. As you travel, keep listening to the radio for additional information and instructions from your local government. Watch out for washed-out or undermined roadways, earth slides, broken sewers or water mains, loose or downed electric wires, and falling or fallen objects. Watch out for areas where rivers or streams may flood suddenly. Do not try to cross a stream or pool of water unless you are certain that the water will not rise above your knees (or above the middle of your car's wheels) all the way across

4 Board up your windows so they will not be broken by high winds, water, flying objects or debris

5 DO NOT stack sandbags around the outside walls of your house to keep flood waters out of your basement...pressure could damage the walls

2 Follow the instructions and advice of your local government

3 Secure your home before leaving

to listen for and how to stock up on essential supplies. As well as practical information, the manual seeks to create the right mindset: people who panic are likely to make mistakes, so the most important thing to do is to remain calm. Crucially, the manual also warns of the risks immediately after a natural disaster, such as damaged buildings, gas leaks and live electrical cables. It further provides tips on obtaining food, clothing and accommodation after the danger has passed.

Advice for tornados

1 When a tornado watch is announced, this means that tornados are expected in or near your area. Keep your radio or television tuned to a local station for information and advice from your local government or weather bureau. Keep watching the sky, especially to the south and south-west. When a tornado watch is announced during the approach of a hurricane, however, keep watching the sky to the east. If you see any revolving, funnel-shaped clouds, report them by telephone immediately to your local police department, sheriff's office or weather bureau

2 Take shelter immediately. Your best protection is an underground shelter or cave, or a substantial steel-framed or reinforced concrete building

5 If you are outside in open country, drive away from the tornado's path, at a right angle to it. If there is not time to do this – or if you are walking – take cover and lie flat in the nearest depression, such as a ditch, culvert excavation [water channel] or ravine

3 Take cover under a sturdy workbench or table

4 Leave open doors and windows on the side of your house away from the tornado, to reduce damage to the building

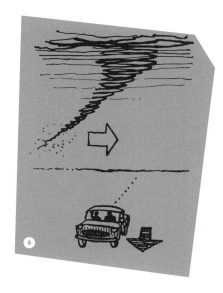

Advice for winter storms

1. Drive with all possible caution. Do not try and save time by travelling faster than road and weather conditions permit. Do not be daring or foolhardy. Stop, turn back or seek help if conditions threaten that may test your ability or endurance. If you are caught in a blizzard, seek refuge immediately

4. If your car breaks down during a storm, do not panic. Think the problem through. Decide what is the safest and best thing to do, and then do it slowly and carefully. If you are on a well-travelled road, show a trouble signal. Stay in your car and wait for help to arrive. If you run the engine to keep warm, open a window wide enough to provide ventilation to protect you from carbon monoxide poisoning

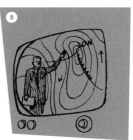

2. Keep up to date on weather conditions. Use your radio, television and newspapers to stay informed of current weather conditions

3. Have emergency winter storm supplies in the car, such as a container of sand, shovel, windshield scraper, tow chain or rope, extra fuel and flashlight

5. Keep an adequate supply of heating fuel on hand and use it sparingly. If necessary, conserve fuel by closing off some rooms temporarily. Also have available some kind of emergency heating equipment and fuel so you can keep at least one room of your house warm enough to live in

Timely Tips When Disaster Strikes, Judge Sherman G. Finesilver, USA, 1969

These tips were designed to help people ensure the safety of themselves, their families and their property under hurricane conditions. The author encourages the disaster-ready citizen not to spread rumours, and instead to stay tuned to their television or radio for live information.

1 Have your car serviced, keep your fuel tank filled... check battery and tyres

2 Have on hand a flashlight, first-aid kit, fire extinguisher and battery-powered radio

3 Keep a supply of drinking water. Stock up on foods that need no cooking or refrigeration

4 Store all loose objects: toys, tools, trash cans, awnings, etc. Board or tape up all windows

5 Move away from low areas that may be hit by storm tides or floods

During the storm:

- STAY INDOORS. Don't be fooled if the calm 'eye' passes directly overhead... and don't be caught in the open when the hurricane winds resume from the OPPOSITE direction
- Listen to your radio or television for information from the weather bureau, civil defence, Red Cross and other authorities

After the storm has passed:

- DO NOT DRIVE unless necessary. Watch out for undermined pavements and broken power lines
- Report downed power lines, broken water or sewer pipes to proper authorities or the nearest policeman
- Use extreme caution to prevent an outbreak of fire or injuries from falling objects
- Use the telephone for emergencies only. Jammed switchboards prevent emergency calls from going through

STAY AWAY FROM DISASTER AREAS

KEEP CALM

FAILURE TO FOLLOW THESE COMMON-SENSE INSTRUCTIONS MAY BRING DANGER

Tornado, US Department of Commerce, USA, 1973

Tornados can form quickly and unexpectedly, so forecasters rely on observers on the ground to spot and report them. In the 1970s, the US authorities received help from thousands of ordinary citizens and police officers involved with nearly 500 community-led SKYWARN networks

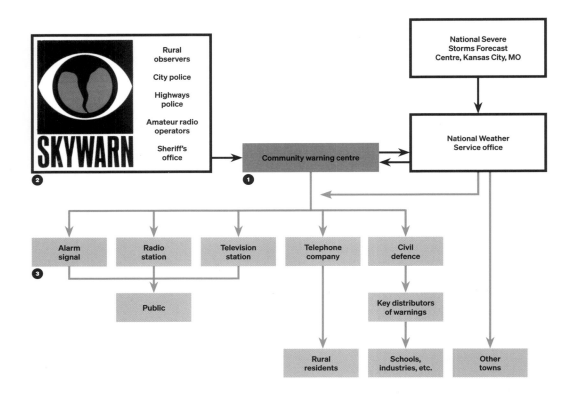

❶ Set up a community warning centre. This is an office that is open at all times – like a police station or telephone exchange – to receive National Weather Service watches and warnings. The community warning centre also receives reports of approaching tornados from local observers and issues local warnings. When a tornado is sighted, the centre notifies nearby towns in the path of the tornado and telephones the nearest office of the National Weather Service so that other areas can be warned ❷ Set up a SKYWARN observer network. Everyone living within 32 km (20 mi) of the community warning centre should know that they should promptly report any observed

tornado to the community warning centre
❸ Set up warning signals. When a tornado is reported locally, a prearranged alarm is sounded. This can be the city fire alarm or civil defence siren. Farmers in threatened areas are warned by telephone, and radio and television stations broadcast the alarm. Keep the alarm system functional. Trial runs and public reminders should be made at regular intervals to ensure a trained, efficient unit is in operation

① A police officer reports a tornado by radio, as part of the SKYWARN warning system.

across the country. SKYWARN volunteers were trained to watch out for warning signs and report any tornados back to the National Weather Service. Vital information, such as the kind of storm, its location, intensity and direction of travel, would be relayed back to the appropriate authorities, allowing them to issue prompt warnings and accurately plot the course of each storm. The only compensation SKYWARN volunteers received for their efforts was 'the certain knowledge that their work saves lives'.

①

The formation of a tornado

The formation of a tornado requires the presence of layers of air with contrasting characteristics of temperature, moisture, density and wind flow. Complicated energy transformations produce the tornado vortex.

Many theories have been postulated regarding the type of energy transformation necessary to generate a tornado, and none has won general acceptance. The two most frequently encountered visualize tornado generation as either the effect of thermally induced rotary circulations, or the effect of converging rotary winds. Currently, scientists seem to agree that neither process generates tornados independently. It is more probable that tornados are produced by the combined effects of thermal and mechanical forces, with one or other force being the stronger generating agent.

❶ THERMAL. Tornado formation is the result of forces set up by the imbalance created when cool air overrides warm air. The imbalance is compensated by rapid upward convection from the lower layers of warm air, which becomes a rotary flow and forms the tornado vortex

❷ THE WORK OF WIND AND PRESSURE. As tornado-velocity winds rip at the exterior of a house, the air inside the house expands explosively into the near-vacuum of the tornado vortex. The combined effects of wind and vacuum produce the near-total destruction of a tornado's progress through populated areas

❸ MECHANICAL. Slowly rotating air currents are constrained by external forces. As the radius of rotation lessens, the speed of rotation increases, in the same way that an ice skater increases their speed of rotation by drawing in their arms. Ultimately, these converging, accelerating, rotary winds set up the tornado vortex

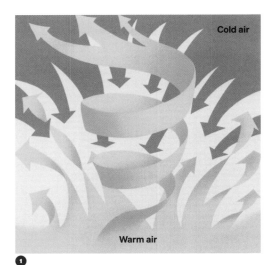

Cold air

Warm air

❶

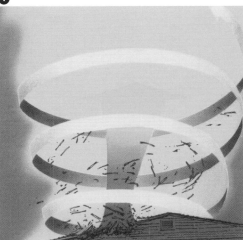

❷

❸

Many tornados only affect a small area and only last for a short time. But, for communities where tornados are common, the sheer violence and destructive force of this class of storm means that understanding them can be the difference between life and death. The simple and clear guidance on these pages was created by the US government to give people some insight into how and why tornados form, and what to look out for.

The life cycle of a tornado

Tornados are local storms of short duration, formed by winds rotating at very high speeds, usually in a counter-clockwise direction. These storms are visible as a vortex: a whirlpool structure of winds rotating about a hollow cavity in which centrifugal forces produce a partial vacuum. As condensation occurs around the vortex, a pale cloud appears: the familiar and frightening tornado funnel. Air surrounding the funnel is also part of the tornado vortex. As the storm moves along the ground, this outer ring of rotating winds becomes dark with dust and debris, which may eventually darken the entire funnel.

1 From a thunderstorm cloud formation, a tornado funnel forms

2 [The tornado funnel] starts towards the surface

3 It then lifts and almost disappears before descending to the ground

4 The same funnel lifts once more

5 It then descends as a second funnel begins to form

6 The second funnel becomes better defined

7 It finally dissipates as the main funnel begins to lengthen

8 Eventually, it disappears

Twister! Tornado Tips to Save Your Life, Illinois Emergency Services and Disaster Agency, USA, 1983

Because it is difficult to know when and where a tornado will land, it is important that everyone knows the safety drills – even children. The Illinois Emergency Services and Disaster Agency produced this flyer for children, with cartoons showing the

❶ Tornados are frequently accompanied by lightning, and lightning can be a killer, too. Here are a few tips from the National Weather Service to protect you when lightning threatens:

- Try and get inside a house or other building or inside an all-metal vehicle. Avoid using the telephone, except for emergencies
- If you are caught outside and have not got time to reach a safe building or car, go to a low place such as a ravine or valley. Be alert for flash floods. In a forest, find shelter in a low area under a thick growth of small trees
- Avoid standing in small, isolated sheds or other small structures in open areas
- A tall tree acts like a lightning rod. Avoid tall, isolated trees in open areas. Do not stand where you project above the surrounding landscape, such as on a hilltop, in a field, on a beach or in a small boat. Stay away from open water
- Avoid the following: tractors and other metal farm equipment, motorcycles, golf carts, bicycles, golf clubs, wire fences, clothes lines and metal pipes, rails or other metallic items that could carry lightning to you from some distance away

TWiSTER!
TORNADO TIPS TO SAVE YOUR LIFE.

Illinois Emergency Services and Disaster Agency

❶

actions to take if tornado-breeding conditions are forecast. It explains how to take shelter if a warning is issued, and how to protect yourself from the lightning strikes that commonly accompany tornados. The flyer also advises children on how to act if they are at home, in school, at a shopping centre or in a car. Children were encouraged to share the information with other family members by posting the flyer in a prominent place at home.

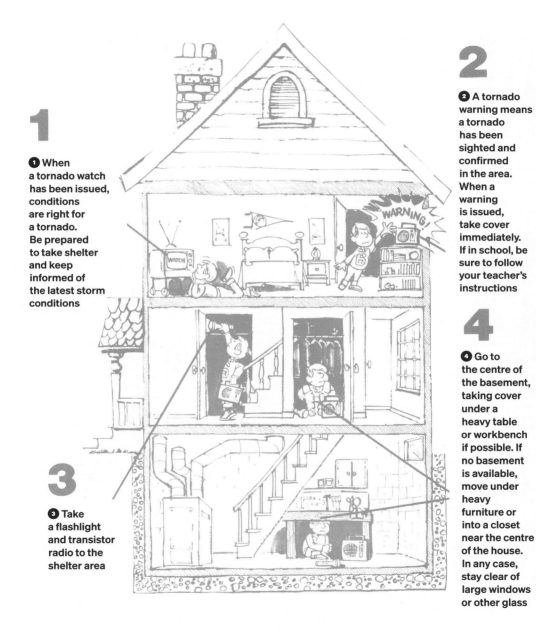

1

❶ When a tornado watch has been issued, conditions are right for a tornado. Be prepared to take shelter and keep informed of the latest storm conditions

2

❷ A tornado warning means a tornado has been sighted and confirmed in the area. When a warning is issued, take cover immediately. If in school, be sure to follow your teacher's instructions

3

❸ Take a flashlight and transistor radio to the shelter area

4

❹ Go to the centre of the basement, taking cover under a heavy table or workbench if possible. If no basement is available, move under heavy furniture or into a closet near the centre of the house. In any case, stay clear of large windows or other glass

Flood Damage Reduction Manual, US Army Corps of Engineers, USA, 1984

These illustrations were produced by the US Army Corps of Engineers as part of a reference manual on measures to reduce damage from floods. They show the steps that building owners can take to flood-proof their properties, and how to drain

Flood proofing

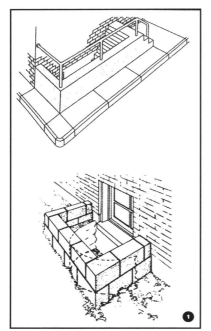

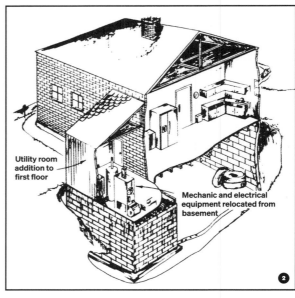

Utility room addition to first floor

Mechanic and electrical equipment relocated from basement

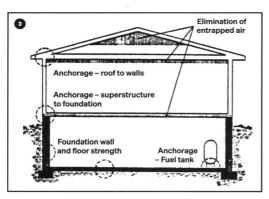

Elimination of entrapped air

Anchorage – roof to walls

Anchorage – superstructure to foundation

Foundation wall and floor strength

Anchorage – Fuel tank

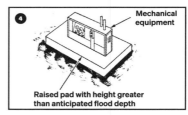

Mechanical equipment

Raised pad with height greater than anticipated flood depth

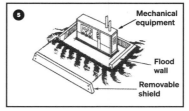

Mechanical equipment

Flood wall

Removable shield

1 Flood-proofing: Low wall around openings

2 Flood-proofing: Relocation of residential, mechanical and electrical equipment to first floor

3 Flood-resistant construction: Critical areas for prevention of structural failure

4 Flood-proofing: Equipment raised on pad

5 Flood-proofing: Low wall around equipment

water out of flooded homes. The manual provides a wide range of emergency measures to reduce the adverse effects of flooding and to deal with the aftermath. Although it could be used as a practical guide in an emergency situation, this manual was more suitable for training purposes. For those on the ground actually dealing with flood damage, a companion publication, the *Flood Fight Field Manual*, provided more instantly practicable advice. The two manuals were intended to complement each other.

Emergency interior drainage

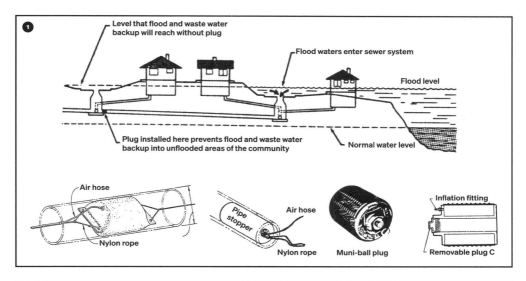

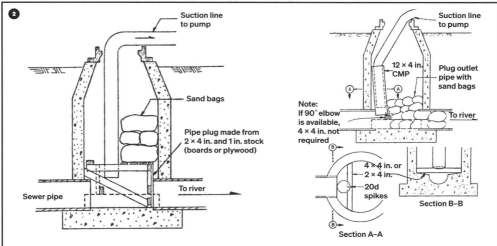

❶ Emergency interior drainage: Pipe stopper. Plug installation (above) and types of plug (below)

❷ Emergency interior drainage: Adapting manhole for pumping

Civil Defence (*Гражданская оборона*), Soviet Union, 1986

Citizens, civil defence workers and 'other forces' work together in these Soviet-era illustrations to cope with the effects of flooding on a rural community. Military vehicles, including a helicopter and an amphibious vehicle, can be seen participating in the relief effort.

1 Rescue and emergency recovery operations in the event of a flood: surveying the flooded area; search and rescue operations; administering first aid to the injured; rescue teams patrolling the flooded area; rescuing livestock, valuables and machinery; carrying out engineering and other measures to reduce the flooded area; increasing the longevity of hydraulic facilities; eliminating blockages

1

2 Rescue efforts during floods are performed by civil defence units, water crews and any other forces and means at the disposal of local authorities

2

The Thames Barrier, Greater London Council, UK, 1980s

The Thames Barrier is a large flood defence structure in London. Before the barrier was built, large areas of the UK capital were at risk from flooding each year. London's councils and transport authorities issued flood warning advice until the early 1980s.

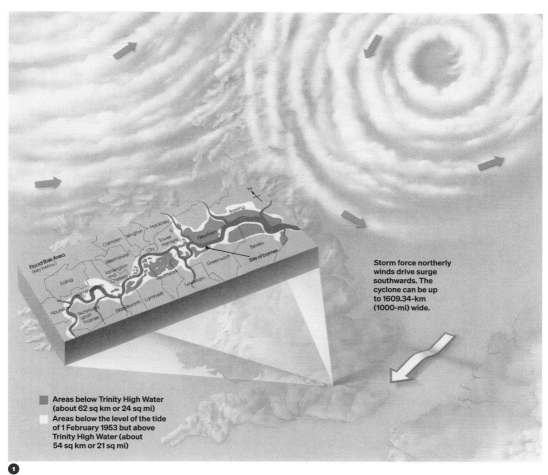

Storm force northerly winds drive surge southwards. The cyclone can be up to 1609.34-km (1000-mi) wide.

- Areas below Trinity High Water (about 62 sq km or 24 sq mi)
- Areas below the level of the tide of 1 February 1953 but above Trinity High Water (about 54 sq km or 21 sq mi)

1

1 How the storm surge develops **2** London flooding is a real danger: Know the flood drill: Ask your town hall or employer **3** What might have happened! **4** GLC Thames Barrier – flood defence for London

Advanced Spotters' Field Guide, US Department of Commerce, USA, 1993

While weather authorities have a vast array of technologies at their disposal – including radar, satellites and lightning detectors – and a clutch of in-house meteorologists, nothing is more important when detecting and reporting extreme weather than trained eyes on the skies. The US National Weather

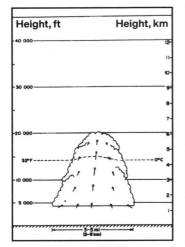

1 Towering cumulus stage of the thunderstorm. At this time, all air is moving upwards in the developing storm

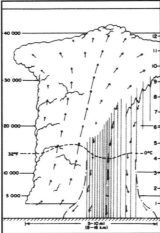

2 Mature stage of the thunderstorm. Updraft and downdraft are coexisting in the storm at this time

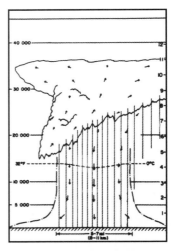

3 Dissipating stage of the thunderstorm. Updraft has weakened and the storm is dominated by downdraft

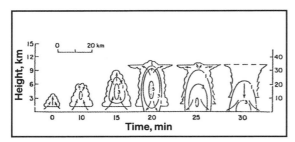

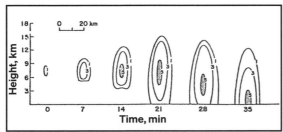

4 Cloud outlines and radar intensity of a single cell storm (top) and radar intensity of a 'pulse' severe storm (bottom)

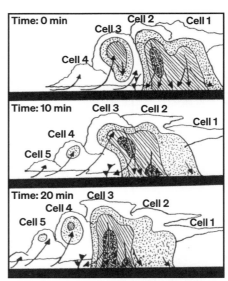

5 Propagation of a multicell cluster storm. Cloud outlines and radar echo intensities are shown

Service provided training for 'spotters', who could provide real-time local weather observations to supplement the more general information obtained from radar. Thanks to the combined efforts of meteorologists and observers, the latter half of the 20th century saw advances in understanding extreme weather. This manual was provided to spotters to give them the latest information on how storms formed and the weather patterns they should look out for.

6 Schematic diagram of a multicell cluster storm. Cloud outlines, radar intensities and the area of greatest severe weather probability are shown

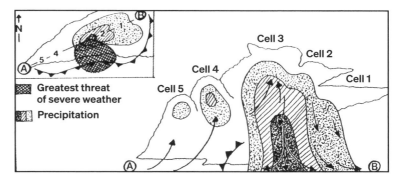

7 Schematic diagram of a squall line. Cloud outlines, radar intensities and the area of greatest severe weather/ tornado threat are shown. Cross-section (left) and overhead (right)

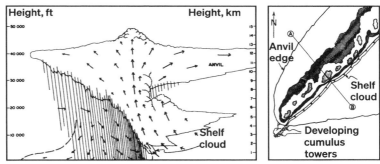

8 Schematic diagram of a bow echo. Strong downburst winds accelerate a portion of the storm, producing the bow or comma echo configurations shown

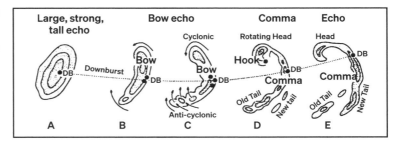

9 Life cycle of a microburst (left), and overhead view of a supercell storm. The precipitation area, gust front and cloud features are shown (right)

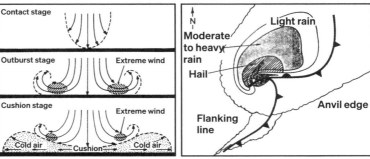

When the Earth Moves

Unlike floods caused by heavy rain, there is very little advance warning of a tsunami. Caused when an earthquake or volcanic eruption below the sea displaces a large volume of water, tsunamis are far more likely to occur near fault lines, primarily in Oceania, Indonesia and Japan, as well as along eastern Asian and western US coasts. In these places, as with tornados, the public must learn the warning signs: an earthquake that lasts a long time, a roaring noise and – most ominously – water suddenly and rapidly being drawn away from the shore. This last feature has proven to be an additional challenge to public safety, as people's natural curiosity means many stay to watch the unusual water movements rather than immediately seeking safety. This reaction is compounded by the normalcy bias: the belief that 'it couldn't happen to me'. In an attempt to combat this counterintuitive behaviour, tsunami hot spots now prominently display hazard notices, with advice to evacuate at once to higher ground should you spot any of the danger signs.

UNESCO operates a global tsunami warning system and runs the International Tsunami Information Centre, which offers public education programmes and coordinates World Tsunami Awareness Day (5 November). Authorities in areas at greater risk of tsunamis take public education seriously, too. Since the 1990s, for example, Hawaii holds a Tsunami Awareness Month each April.

Like tsunamis, volcanoes are primarily found along the Earth's major fault lines and can strike without warning, causing untold destruction and loss of life in mere moments. The 20th century's worst volcanic disaster – the eruption of Martinique's Mount Pelée in 1902 – killed 30,000 people in just 60 seconds. The pyroclastic flow – a swirling, fast-moving torrent of rock, ash and gas – engulfed the bustling city of Saint-Pierre almost instantly, leaving only two survivors: a prisoner, saved by the bomb-proof cell where he was being held, and another man who is thought to have been in the sea when the deadly flow hit. The catastrophe at Saint-Pierre

① Houses in San Francisco tilt precariously after the 1906 earthquake. ② The San Francisco earthquake damaged roads and left tram lines bent out of shape. ③ A man walks through the wreckage following the 1906 San Francisco quake. ④ Men salvage valuable materials from a ruined rum distillery after the eruption of Mount Pelée, Martinique, in 1902.

Overleaf:

⑤⑥⑦⑧ Popular children's characters Yogi Bear and Boo Boo helped teach kids how to act during an earthquake. Yogi, who famously claimed to be 'smarter than the average bear', also starred in an animated short film on earthquake preparedness. He even showed children how to prepare an emergency kit, shown here as a handy picnic basket.

①

②

③

④

demonstrates the need for serious public education in areas where active volcanoes pose a threat.

As with any education programme about natural disasters, governments must find a way to retain public confidence in volcano alert systems and avoid creating a lack of trust. With an active volcano, there is an added risk that those living in its shadow may become complacent (the normalcy bias again) and ignore the warning signs until it is too late.

Activity at Mount Pinatubo in the Philippines in 1991 suggested to volcanologists that it was preparing to erupt on an unprecedented scale, and they recommended evacuating some 200,000 people from the area. The Filipino authorities found themselves balancing the risk of a false alarm – which would seriously dent faith in future warnings – against the potential for massive loss of life should the volcanologists be proven right. In the event, the timely warnings and evacuation plan meant that, although more than 800 people died, many thousands of lives were saved. The eruption at Mount Pinatubo sent a cubic mile of material into the air, resulting in an ash cloud some 35 km (22 mi) high, in what was the largest volcanic eruption since 1912.

Earthquakes represent another great tectonic threat to human life. In Japan, resilience against earthquakes is built not only into the structure of homes and offices, but also into the fabric of society. From a technological standpoint, the country has invested in innovation to ensure minimal damage occurs to buildings. Equally, however, preparedness is woven into daily life: public alert systems are tested regularly, routes for emergency vehicles are well-marked, and information on evacuation plans is issued to everyone. Radio stations are teed up to broadcast information not only in Japanese, but also in a wide variety of languages. Property companies even issue advice on surviving earthquakes to renters and homeowners.

Weaving earthquake preparedness into society has also benefited people in Chile, where the death toll from powerful earthquakes has been many times lower than in less well-organized countries. Again, this has been put down to more than just investment in buildings. When an earthquake strikes, warning systems keep the public well-informed, but, critically, the government ensures that the public is already familiar with disaster preparedness advice and evacuation plans before a quake hits.

Governments in earthquake zones around the world also issue more traditional advice in the form of earthquake drills. New Zealand's Civil Defence organization, for example, advises people to 'Drop, cover and hold' – drop to the floor, to avoid being knocked over; cover your head and neck; and hold onto your shelter.

There is one final tectonic disaster for which there can be no realistic preparation: the supervolcano. Yellowstone National Park in the United States is home to Yellowstone Caldera, a vast area of more than

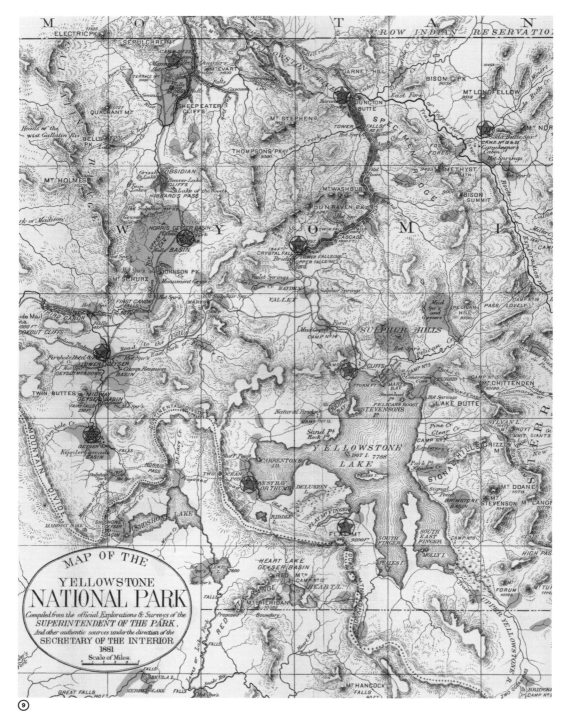

⑨

⑨ This map of Yellowstone National Park in the western United States shows the locations of known geysers and hot springs at the turn of the century.

We now know that geysers are a symptom of the geological danger lurking beneath the surface.

3,000 sq km (1,200 sq mi), below which sits a build-up of magma, held barely below the surface. This 'hot spot' is responsible for the park's famous hot springs and geysers: geothermal features such as 'Old Faithful', which delight tourists by spraying naturally heated water high into the air each day. The last time the supervolcano erupted – some 640,000 years ago – it ejected around 1,000 cu km (240 cu mi) of material. By comparison, the 1883 eruption at Krakatoa, Indonesia, sent just 25 cu km (6 cu mi) flying.

A supervolcano eruption would wreak utter devastation on the world's climate. While scientists do not believe we are due one any time soon, the magma below the Yellowstone Caldera continues to raise the ground level by several inches every year.

⑩

⑪

⑩ ⑪ The geysers caused by the Yellowstone Caldera means the park could be a dangerous excursion for an unwary tourist. This pamphlet,

Danger: Your Safety? Hazards in Yellowstone National Park (1983 and 1975) advised visitors on the risks of straying from designated paths.

Earthquake safety propaganda posters, Dizhen chubanshe, China, 1976

The earthquake at Tangshan in 1976 rocked China politically. The ruling Maoist politicians, known as the 'Gang of Four' downplayed the disaster, which claimed more than 242,000 lives. Three months later, they were arrested, bringing to an end the Cultural Revolution period.

① 深入批邓 抗震救灾

② 地震不足畏 人民定胜天

③ 加强党的领导发挥共产党员共青团员模范带头作用

④ 战斗的号召 光辉的榜样

① This poster calls for criticism of the Gang of Four's handling of the earthquake. ② This poster proclaims that 'earthquakes cannot frighten us, the people will certainly conquer nature'. ③ Using the earthquake in Tangshan as context, this poster encourages strengthening party leadership using the youth as role models. ④ This poster references Hua Guofeng's (a critic of the Gang of Four) visit to a coal mine in Tangshan, months after the earthquake there. ⑤ This relief poster carries the message that 'socialism is best' as the whole nation supports a disaster-stricken area. ⑥ The smiling group on this poster are accompanied by the message that the country is united in preparation and prevention.

⑤

⑥

Learning to Live in Earthquake Country: Preparedness for People with Disabilities, Federal Emergency Management Agency, USA, 1984

1 Earthquakes are part of the process that shapes the surface of the Earth, raising mountains and deepening valleys

2 Electricity, water, telephone and natural gas services could be severely damaged, leaving areas without utilities for days, perhaps weeks

3 Your main source of help after an earthquake will be your neighbours. Get to know them

4 Your family should have a home evacuation plan – a plan that is usable for both fire and earthquake dangers

5 Have at least 20 l (5 gal) of water per person in plastic bottles in a safe place. Change it every six months

6 Knowledge of first aid is essential after a large earthquake, as medical facilities may be damaged or overcrowded

7 A fire extinguisher, type ABC, belongs in every home... after an earthquake it may be needed to put out small fires

8 If you are dependent on electrical power for life support or require an electric wheelchair, buy a small generator

9 Keep flashlights around the house, including one next to the bed, and at work, with extra batteries

10 To get information on food, water and evacuation areas after an earthquake, keep a radio handy, with extra batteries

11 You are going to need to walk over broken glass and other debris. Keep a pair of thick-soled shoes and work gloves under your bed

12 What are the things you rely on to get along? You should have at least an extra week's supply of these things on hand

This publication aims to help disabled people living in 'earthquake country' take steps to protect themselves and their loved ones. It encourages people to create neighbourhood and family earthquake plans that take into account the needs of disabled community members. It highlights the difficulties that wheelchair users may face if corridors become obstructed with debris, and that vision-impaired people may encounter in the unfamiliar surroundings of damaged buildings. It also notes that household objects, such as heavy items on shelves, can become unstable after a quake.

13 Find cover. Move away from windows, high furniture and other dangers. Move to an interior doorway or under heavy furniture

14 Check for gas leaks. If you smell gas, shut off your gas at the meter, or have someone else do it

15 If you are trapped after an earthquake, do anything you can to attract attention

16 Beware of heavy objects on high shelves, hanging plants, furniture and things on walls

17 Beware of cupboards (jars, cans, pots and pans could be heading your way)

18 Remove heavy objects from high shelves or secure them. Remove any heavy object from above your bed

19 Secure hanging plants. Make sure they are either screwed into wood or, in the case of plaster or drywall, use an appropriate fastener

20 Secure top-heavy furniture to the wall with eye-screws and L-brackets

21 Secure pictures and mirrors

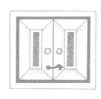

22 Secure cupboards. Attractive positive-close latches are available at most hardware stores

23 Secure appliances. Even something as heavy as a refrigerator could scoot around or even tip over during an earthquake

24 Secure your water heater. When full, a 150-l (40-gal) water heater weighs well over 136 kg (300 lb)

Family Earthquake Safety: Home Hazard Hunt and Drill, Federal Emergency Management Agency, USA, 1986

This guide provides all the information people need to ensure they can fully prepare for an earthquake. It features a 'Hazard Hunt' section to help people identify potential dangers in their homes, such as heavy furniture and flying glass.

FEMA 113 / September 1986
(Supersedes FEMA 47 and FEMA 49 which may be used)

FAMILY EARTHQUAKE SAFETY HOME HAZARD HUNT AND DRILL

 American Red Cross ✚

①

1 Be prepared to deal with the emotional needs of family members. Stay close enough to touch and comfort each other

2 Secure gas lines by installing flexible connectors to appliances

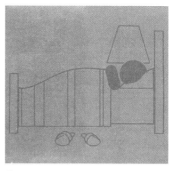

3 At night, keep a pair of shoes by your bed to protect your feet from broken glass and other debris

4 Look at the floor-to-ceiling bookcase: how much stuff would fall off the shelves? Will the whole bookcase topple or is it anchored to the wall?

5 Stand or crouch in a strong supported doorway

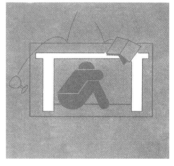

6 Get under a sturdy table or desk, or brace yourself in an inside corner of the house

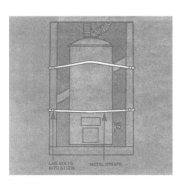

7 Thin metal straps, known as 'plumber's tape', can be used to fasten your hot water heater to the wood studs of the nearest wall

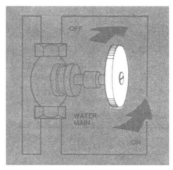

8 If you smell gas, get to the gas and water mains and turn them off

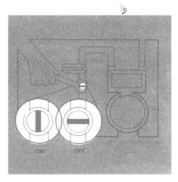

9 Do not light matches or candles to look for damage

① *Family Earthquake Safety: Home Hazard Hunt and Drill*, 1986, front cover.

Civil Defence
(Гражданская оборона),
Soviet Union, 1986

This Soviet civil defence guide shows the expected response to an earthquake hitting an urban area. Potential hazards include fires, ruined buildings and danger from collapsed electricity pylons and overhead cables. The risk of disease is also highlighted.

1

① During an earthquake of enormous strength, energy ripples out in the form of seismic waves. An earthquake can last anywhere from a few seconds to a few days (recurring tremors)... The highest priority rescue and emergency recovery operations at the epicentre of earthquakes are: **②** Conducting searches of the affected areas; finding and rescuing the injured from fallen rubble; rescuing people from partially destroyed buildings and buildings on fire **③** Administering first aid to the injured and evacuating them to medical facilities

④ Putting out fires **⑤** Creating passages through the rubble to enable access to target sites; razing or reinforcing unstable structures and buildings; localizing and eliminating damage to utility networks; evacuating people to safer areas; establishing and equipping evacuation centres and medical centres; providing victims with water, food and clothing; organizing water supply centres; setting up security services; collecting and guarding valuables; carrying out anti-epidemic measures

②

③

④

⑤

Earthquakes and Preparedness: Before, During and After, Earthquake Preparedness Society, USA, 1989

Before

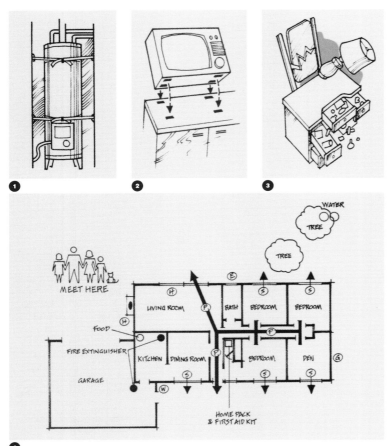

① Securely strap the hot water heater at the top and bottom ② Quake Grip from Velcro USA is a speciality hook and lock fastener for home safety application that may hold items in place ③ Possessions that you enjoy and love may become deadly flying objects during a major earthquake ④ Use the enclosed tear-out in the centre of the book to sketch your floor plan. Include the following key points: primary (P) and secondary (S) exit routes from each room; safest place to take cover in each room; mark hazards (H); storage area for water, food, first-aid kit, home pack etc.; location of fire extinguishers; outside 'meet here' area; location of electrical (E), gas (G) and water (W) service shut-offs ⑤ Put together a three- to five-day emergency home pack for each individual. Place the supplies in one bag stored close to an exit

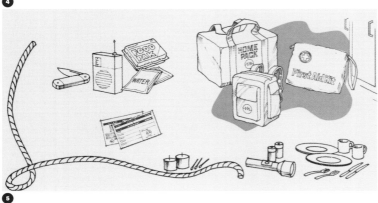

This comprehensive manual is a one-stop shop for the cautious citizen. It is packed with checklists and diagrams for preparing your home, creating an earthquake plan and knowing what to expect should the worst happen. It includes a suggested emergency kit and space for sketching a home floor plan. It provides emergency contact cards that can be torn out and kept by each family member. These allow an out-of-state family member or friend to be nominated as a central point of contact, ensuring families can keep in touch even if they are in different locations when the earthquake strikes.

During

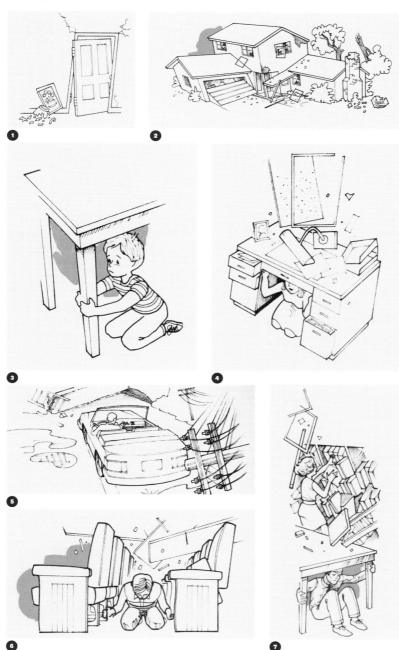

❶ Door frames may bend ❷ Most wood-frame and stucco homes or buildings tend to stand up to earthquakes well. If your home is unreinforced brick or other masonry, it may not withstand a severe earthquake ❸ If you are inside, try and take cover under a table or other sturdy furniture. Kneel, sit or stay close to the floor. Hold onto furniture legs for balance. Be prepared to move with your cover ❹ If you choose to go under a table or desk, hold on tightly ❺ If you are in a bus or car, stop your vehicle. Stay inside the vehicle during and after the earthquake. In most situations, it is a safe place to be ❻ If you are in a theatre, auditorium or public place, stay in your seat, get low and ride the earthquake out ❼ One of the most common causes of earthquake injury is panic. Many earthquake injuries are sustained when people panic and try to run outside or to another area of the building. Objects as small as an ashtray or as large as a television may become airborne

After

1 Think before you move! Remain in a safe position until shaking stops. Move slowly and carefully. Many serious injuries are caused by inappropriate actions, not collapsing buildings **2** Using swimming pools for drinking water over an extended period of time may cause physical damage **3** There are three major types of fire: usual combustibles (cloth, paper, many plastics, rubber and wood), flammable liquids (gasoline, kitchen greases, oils, paint, lacquer and solvent) and electrical equipment (fuse, boxes, motors, power tools, appliances and wires) **4** Check for fires. Extinguish them while they are small. Use a fire extinguisher, available water or even dirt to put out fires. If unable to extinguish the fire, evacuate immediately **5** Turn off electricity at fuse box or circuit breaker panel. At circuit breaker panel, first switch off small breakers, then large ones. At fuse box, first unscrew fuses, then turn off main **6** To improve the taste of stored water, you could expose it to fresh air or pour it several times from one container to another

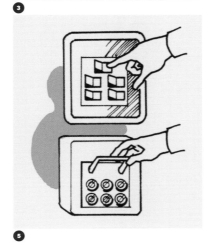

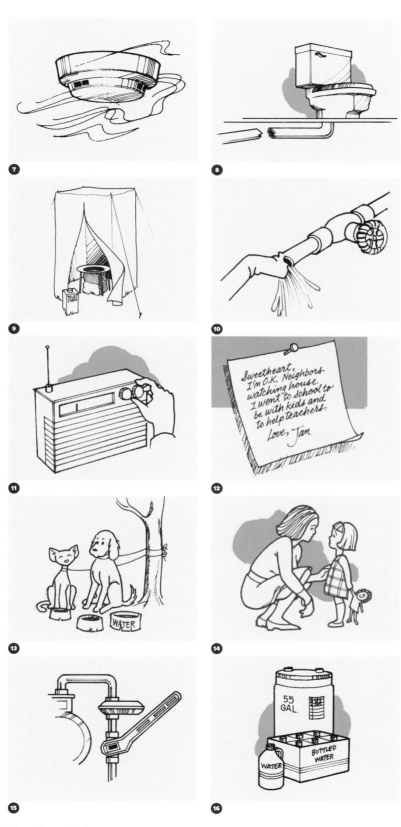

7 Normally, when you have a fire it is best to call the fire department. However, after a severe earthquake the phones may be out of service. Or the fire department may be overwhelmed and unable to respond for a delayed period of time. You may have to fight your own fire **8** Before using toilets or sinks, check the surrounding neighbourhood to see if sewer and water pipes are intact. If your toilet is flushed, raw sewage could be dumped in your neighbour's yard **9** If sewer pipes are damaged, empty the toilet bowl and line it with a heavy plastic bag **10** Water service: make sure valves are free turning **11** Stay put and turn on your radio to listen for advice. Cooperate with public safety efforts **12** Upon evacuation, leave a written message. State your destination and route of travel **13** Pets become nervous after an earthquake. Confine them so they do not get away and hurt themselves or others. Give them food, water and an area to sleep **14** Young children and senior citizens tend to be more susceptible to emotional stress from an earthquake than other age groups **15** After an earthquake, turn the gas off if you smell, hear or even suspect gas is escaping **16** Store bulk drinking water outside in new or used high-density plastic barrels

Civil Defence poster campaign, Ministry of Civil Defence, New Zealand, 1980s

These posters were created to educate the public on disaster preparedness. Practical measures include keeping a portable radio handy, maintaining a survival kit and packing a 'disaster getaway kit'. However, the campaign does not only focus on the individual: posters also encourage people to be community-spirited and help vulnerable neighbours.

❶

1 Your Disaster Getaway Kit: Family documents such as birth and marriage certificates and insurance policies; extra clothing; towels and toilet items; essential medicines; baby needs; blankets and food, if possible **2** Civil Defence: People Helping People. In major emergencies, civil defence has three goals: to prevent loss of lives, to help the injured and to relieve personal suffering **3** In A Disaster... Give a Thought for Your Neighbours **4** Always Keep Your Battery Radio Alive and Healthy. In a disaster, it could do the same for you! Check it regularly **5** Your Disaster Survival Kit: Keep it ready, keep it complete at all times

CIVIL DEFENCE
People Helping People

In major emergencies,
Civil Defence has three goals:
to prevent loss of lives,
to help the injured,
to relieve personal suffering.

For more information contact the
Civil Defence Officer at your local Council.

2

IN A DISASTER...
GIVE A THOUGHT FOR YOUR NEIGHBOURS

Act towards your neighbours as you'd hope they'd act towards you.

Read the last Yellow Page of your phone book.

NEIGHBOURS MAY NEED HELP...ESPECIALLY IF THEY'RE ELDERLY, DISABLED, OR HAVE YOUNG CHILDREN.

For more information contact the Civil Defence Officer at your local Council.

3

ALWAYS KEEP YOUR BATTERY RADIO
ALIVE AND HEALTHY

In a disaster it could do the same for you!

In a disaster a battery radio could well be your only way of finding out what is happening, what to do, where to go.

Every household should have at least one battery radio, in first class working order, with spare, fully-charged batteries.

CHECK IT REGULARLY.
See the last Yellow Page of your phone book for detailed advice.

4

YOUR DISASTER SURVIVAL KIT
Keep it ready, keep it complete, at all times.

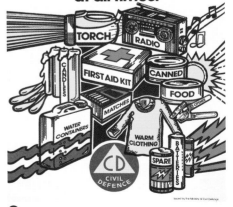

5

Disaster Preparedness Tokyo (東京防災), Tokyo Metropolitan Government, Japan, 2015

Japan is located at the meeting point of several tectonic plates, which means that no part of the country has escaped the ferocious, destructive power of earthquakes. The fact that earthquakes are deeply embedded in the national psyche, combined with Japan's economic success,

❶ If you are in the living room, you must be wary of being trapped under tall furniture that has toppled over, or being injured by broken glass from windows or lighting fixtures. If you feel a tremor, take cover in a place where you will be protected from falling objects or furniture and other heavy items falling over or sliding into you. You should also watch out for things such as large, heavy kitchen appliances, including refrigerators and microwave ovens, as well as items flying off shelves

❷ Copy machines and other office furnishings on unlocked casters can move around the room in an unpredictable manner. You could be severely injured if you are hit by one. You could even be killed if you are hit on the head by flying objects or debris, such as shards of broken glass. While being wary of falling cabinets and shattered glass, you need to move to a safe place to protect yourself from falling objects or furniture and other heavy items toppling over or sliding into you

means the country is now one of the most earthquake-ready nations in the world. The Tokyo Metropolitan Government sent its *Disaster Preparedness Tokyo* pack to 7.5 million homes as part of an effort to encourage disaster preparedness. As well as stickers and maps, the pack included a comprehensive manual that uses engaging cartoon illustrations and manga-style comics to encourage people to prepare for the worst. The campaign also employed a cute hard hat-wearing rhino character who told people: 'Let's get prepared!'

❸ The higher the floor, the stronger the shaking will be. If you are a visitor in a building, remain in a public area, such as the elevator hall, crouch close to the ground and listen for instructions over the public address system

❹ At the earliest, a large tsunami could reach the coastline within minutes. Call out to those around you and promptly move to higher ground. If there is no higher ground in the area, evacuate to a safe location, such as a tsunami evacuation tower

❺ In facilities where a great number of people gather, such as theatres, halls and stadiums, do not rush towards the emergency exit or stairs, but listen to the public address system and follow instructions given by staff

❻ While protecting yourself from falling objects and debris, and watching out for collapsing buildings, move to a safe place such as a park. If you are unable to flee to an open area, take refuge in a relatively new, reinforced concrete building that is seismic resistant. One of the scariest things that can happen in a crowd is the eruption of panic

❼ To protect yourself from flying shards of glass and falling lighting fixtures in the classroom, move away from windows, take cover under a desk, hold onto the desk's legs and wait until the shaking subsides. If you are in the hall, quickly move away from windows; on the stairs, grab hold of the railing to avoid losing your balance and falling. When the shaking stops, follow the instructions given by teachers and staff

❽ In the event of a major disaster such as an earthquake directly hitting the capital, the full efforts of the residents are important to overcome the situation. Do not just think about yourself and your family, but cooperate with those around you and help as many people as possible. This concept of looking out for each other (mutual help) will help mitigate the damage of the earthquake

Volcanoes, Secretary of Security and Citizen Protection, Mexico, 2021

In addition to its west coast forming part of the Pacific 'Ring of Fire' (a region where many earthquakes and volcanoes occur), Mexico is further straddled by the Trans-Mexican Volcanic Belt, a range of volcanoes forming a chain across the country. Perhaps most notable among these

❶ For those who live near an active volcano, this manual provides information about the dangers volcanoes pose and some safety recommendations

❷ What is a volcano? It is an opening in the earth through which magma erupts

❸ When very hot materials accumulate under a volcano, the build-up of pressure and temperature can cause them to spew out in the form of lava, ash, rocks, vapours and gases, producing a volcanic eruption

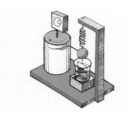

❹ In many cases, it has been possible to predict when a volcano will erupt. For this to occur, a monitoring system is needed

❺ A warning system has been developed for the Popocatépetl volcano. It is known as the Semáforo de Alerta Volcánica

❻ Volcanic eruptions can result in several types of hazards, including mudslides, pyroclastic flows and avalanches

❼ First, identify whether the volcano is active... Next, familiarize yourself with the emergency plans and also the location of a temporary shelter, in case you need to evacuate the area

❽ During periods of volcanic activity, the main hazard is falling ash, as it remains in the air for some time. This can cause irritation to eyes and airways, respiratory problems, and issues with food, drainage, electronic devices, etc.

❾ Ash can cause drains and pipes to become blocked. It is important to sweep the street, pathway and roof to prevent this from happening

is Popocatépetl, a massive active volcano situated less than 80 km (50 mi) from the capital, Mexico City. The ongoing threat of volcanic activity puts the Mexican population in direct danger. Public education, therefore, is a priority for health and safety planners. This manual uses simple illustrations to explain how and why a volcanic eruption occurs, and how to protect your family and property. It also encourages people to trust the authorities and participate in life-saving evacuation plans.

10 Take care of your pets and farm animals. Cover any food, straw or hay with tarpaulins, plastic or sacks. Do not leave anything out in the open. Cover wells to keep water free of ash

11 Remember, if you live in a high danger zone, evacuation before a volcanic eruption is the best course of action to protect yourself and your family

12 In the temporary shelter, identify the members of your family, especially children, the elderly and people with different abilities, noting their name, blood type and other personal information

13 At the end of the emergency, only the authorities can indicate when it is safe to return to home. Do not pay attention to unofficial information

14 Memorize the signage. Signs are very important because they help us to recognize what needs to be done or where to go

15 Evacuation routes indicate the safest streets and paths to follow out of the danger area and towards assembly points or temporary shelters

16 Trucks will arrive at meeting points or centres to move you to a safe place

17 Check out the sites that have been designated to provide you with services and protection during the emergency

Fighting Fire

Fire plays an important role in nature. Some ecosystems rely on wildfires to return vital nutrients to the soil and even to trigger seed germination. These include plants whose seed pods can resist being ravaged by the fire itself, but then crack open to deposit their seeds in the rich ash left behind. Wildfires can also destroy toxins in the soil and transform decaying plant matter on the ground into charcoal, a natural fertilizer.

However, out-of-control wildfires can cause catastrophic devastation not only to vegetation, but also to transport, communications and energy infrastructure. They severely degrade air quality and send vast quantities of greenhouse gases into the atmosphere. Exacerbated by man-made problems such as deforestation and climate change, they destroy crops, homes and businesses; damage animal and plant ecosystems; and injure and kill people.

Wildfires occur globally and can be triggered by natural events, such as lightning strikes, or by human activity, such as unattended campfires, arson, fireworks or discarded cigarettes. Most people imagine wildfires to be forest fires, of the kind seen in US news reports, but they can, in fact, affect any area dense with plants, such as grassland, prairies and peat bogs.

The mechanics of wildfires can be somewhat counterintuitive. The spread of a fire depends on the type of vegetation, and so it can be hard to predict and often impossible to control. For example, bog fires – which occur in places as diverse as Russia, Canada and Borneo – can burn below the ground for long periods before re-emerging in unexpected locations, far from the site of the original blaze. The speed at which wildfires move – known as the 'forward rate of spread' – varies from 10 km/h (6 mph) in forests to as fast as 20 km/h (12.5 mph) in grassland. The latter is about the same speed that a healthy human adult can run. On rare occasions, the intensity of a wildfire can be sufficient to cause a highly destructive 'fire tornado'.

In areas particularly prone to wildfires, authorities plan for outbreaks by creating evacuation routes and

① Firefighters use shovels to defeat a slow-moving 'back fire' in California, 1936.
② An early 20th-century fire truck from Wangaratta, Australia.
③ An Australian soldier fights a bush fire on the outskirts of Sydney, 1964.
④ Men put out a wildfire in South Dakota in the first half of the 20th century.

① ② ③ ④

emergency plans, which can include public shelters to accommodate those forced to leave their homes. They also provide guidance to the public: residents are encouraged to make contingency plans, be aware of official alerts and take steps to increase the safety of their homes. In wildfire hot spots in the United States, people are encouraged to ensure they have a range of supplies – including masks – in their homes at all times. They are advised to arrange access to outdoor water sources and to create a buffer zone of 9 m (30 ft) around their property that is kept free of any flammable materials. As a wildfire approaches, people are advised to turn off gas supplies, put on respirators and soak their property with water – starting with the roof – to prevent airborne embers setting it alight.

Given the tremendous damage a wildfire can cause, authorities also run campaigns to prevent them from occurring in the first place. The US Forest Service's iconic 'Smokey Bear' campaign is perhaps the most prominent public information campaign around wildfire prevention. In fact, it forms part of the 'Wildfire Prevention Campaign', the country's longest-running public service advertising campaign. Smokey Bear's slogan – 'Only YOU can prevent forest fires' – has become deeply embedded in US popular culture since its debut in 1944. At the turn of the century, it was updated to 'Only YOU can prevent wildfires', in order to underline the fact that wildfires are not limited to forests.

Climate change has led to wildfires becoming more destructive and occurring in more places around the world. Changing weather patterns mean once-fertile areas are now drier for longer, and increased storm activity results in more lightning strikes, the primary source of ignition. In 2019, this led to an area of Amazon rainforest more than 9,065 sq km (3,500 sq mi) in size being decimated by tens of thousands of uncontrolled wildfires.

Authorities are increasingly struggling to bring wildfires under control. This uptick has led to something of a vicious circle, with the release of greenhouse gases and particulate matter into the atmosphere – plus the loss of forests and other vegetation – further impacting the climate. Over the coming years, as the spread and severity of wildfires increase further, governments will need to continue to find ways to effectively educate and inform the public on how to cope with this growing threat.

⑤ A poster advertises a public exhibition on fire safety in Paris, June/July 1929.
⑥ France also hosted the third International Fire Exhibition in 1934.
⑦ A French poster from 1939 lists the many causes of house fires and asks: Have you planned for fire?
⑧ A poster advertising a spectacular event featuring fire trucks and helicopters to mark the French National Fire and Civil Protection Day in 1964.

⑤

⑥

⑦

⑧

Forest Fires: How to Fight Them, Commonwealth of Pennsylvania Department of Forestry, USA, 1922

Fires spread through woodland at a rate faster than human walking pace, so there is little time to think when faced with an inferno. It is, therefore, essential that firefighters have tried and tested methods of dealing with forest fires in their arsenal.

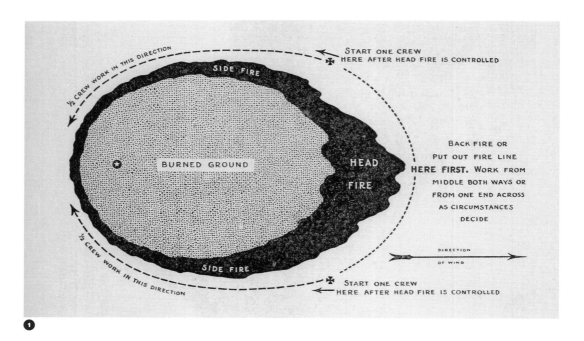

❶

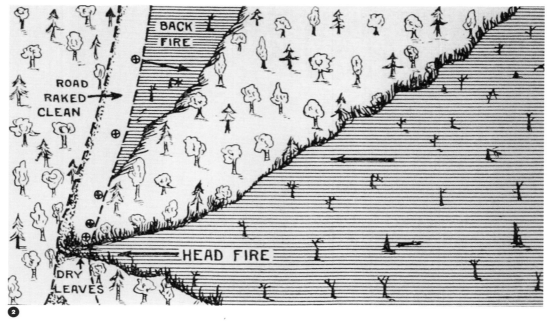

❷

This manual, published in Pennsylvania in 1922, provides the latest tactics for stopping a forest fire in its tracks. As these illustrations show, one of the main variables that governs how a fire behaves is the wind speed and direction. A 'head fire' is one that has the wind behind it, which makes it very difficult to control. The manual also describes the process of 'back firing', in which a fire is intentionally set along the inner edge of a fireline to consume the fuel in the path of a wildfire.

❶ The correct way to attack any forest fire. Always work from the front towards the rear. Stop the head fire first and work far enough to each side so that the side fire cannot work around the edges to make a new head fire ❷ The incorrect way to attack by back fire. The head fire reaches the firebreak and jumps over it before the back fire reaches the point of advantage ❸ Where an angle can be used, the back fire may have to be longer, but the area burnt by the back fire is reduced. Be careful that the side fire does not come up before the wings of the back fire are safe ❹ If working straight across the head fire, the back fire must be long enough to check not only the narrow head fire, but also the full width of the fire behind ❺ Fire observation tower system in Pennsylvania

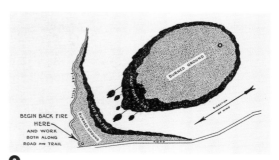

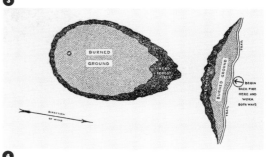

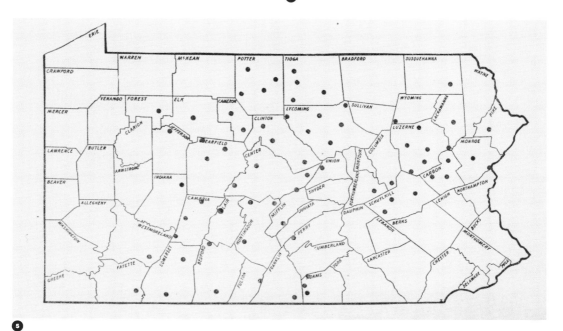

Manual: Forest Fire Fighters Service, Minnesota Office of Civilian Defence, USA, 1942

The easiest way to deal with a forest fire is to ensure that it does not start in the first place. Forest services around the world have long invested heavily in public information work to educate the public about the risks of fire, with some campaigns

Causes

1 Smokers. Be sure that pipe ashes and cigar and cigarette stubs are dead before you throw them away

2 Clearing or burning debris. Never light a fire during windy or dry weather. Never light a fire until late afternoon or evening

3 Incendiarism. Report all suspected cases of incendiarism to the forest office

4 Campfires. When making a campfire, select a spot near water or where there is an abundance of loose mineral earth

Tools

1 Cutter mattock

2 Pulaski tool

3 Double-bit axe

4 Single-bit axe

5 Finn hoe

6 Fire rake

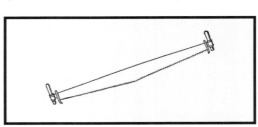

7 Crosscut saw

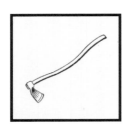

8 Grub hoe

9 Short-handled shovel

10 Round point shovel

11 Back-pack pump

running for many years or even decades. The illustrations here, from a Minnesota Civilian Defence manual, explain some of the causes of forest fires, the main tools used to put them out and the means by which fires can be brought under control. The causes shown here are identified by the manual as the four primary ways that forest fires begin. Some 98 per cent of forest fires are man-made and, therefore, entirely preventable through education and vigilance.

Suppression

❶ Controlling or checking the spread of a forest fire. Hot spotting: This is merely concentrating the initial attack upon those sectors of the edge of the fire that are burning the hardest. Fire control lines: Control lines are natural barriers or constructed line which are used to stop or hold a forest fire. There are four generally recognized methods of control line construction, namely the direct, 2-foot, parallel and indirect. The direct method: as the name implies, this involves direct action on the fire itself... digging out every spark of fire along the edge of the burn. The 2-foot method: This is a substitute for the direct method in those situations where there is a large amount of fuel at the edge of the fire... it usually involves a continuos fire line... not more than 0.6 m (2 ft) from the burning edge of the fire ❷ The indirect method: This consists of completing a continuous fire control line quite a distance in advance of the fire and then back firing ❸ The parallel method: This method consists of constructing a continuous trench somewhat parallel to and within 30.5 m (100 ft) of the edge of the fire, immediately burning out the intervening strip of unburned material

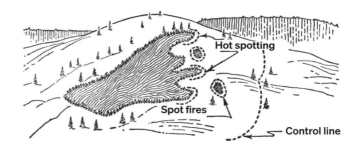

❶

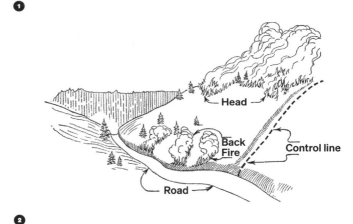

❷

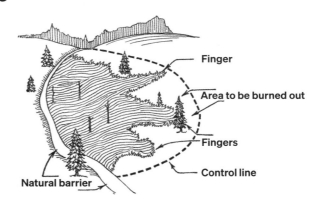

❸

National Security Council Fire Safety Campaign, Australia, 1970–80

A common thread that runs through public fire safety campaigns around the world is the fact that the very tiniest source of ignition – such as a discarded match – can lead to a devastating, out-of-control wildfire. Australia's 'Little Causes

1

Start Big Fires' poster campaign built on this idea, underlining the fact that the majority of forest fires have preventable causes. Another campaign, from around the same period, details the different kinds of fire extinguishers for each type of conflagration – water for dry materials, foam for liquid fires and carbon monoxide for electrical fires – and their methods of deployment. A final poster encourages people to carry fuel in appropriate spill-proof containers rather than in buckets.

❶ Little Causes Start Big Fires ❷ In case of fire: 1. Call the fire brigade 2. Evacuate the area 3. Fight the fire if safe to do so ❸ Flammable liquids: Use a safe container ❹ In case of live electrical equipment fire, use in this way: 1. Carry to scene 2. Remove safety pin 3. Squeeze carrying handle and direct discharge horn at base of fire ❺ In case of flammable liquid fire, use in this way: 1. Carry to scene 2. Place thumb over nozzle and invert extinguisher 3. Direct stream of foam to blanket fire – never into burning liquid ❻ In case of wood, paper, textiles, rubbish fire, use in this way: 1. Carry to scene 2. Place thumb over nozzle and invert extinguisher 3. Direct stream at base of fire then from side to side and around fire

Civil Defence (*Гражданская оборона*), Soviet Union, 1986

This page from an unusually comprehensive Soviet civil defence guide shows trained firefighters using a number of methods to quell the flames, including digging trenches and spraying the fire with high-powered water jets.

❶

❷

1 **2** Fighting forest fires: Throwing soil at or beating the edge of a fire; setting up control lines, barriers and ditches; extinguishing the fire with water or fire-extinguishing chemicals; starting an oncoming fire (back fire) **3** **4** Fighting peat fires: Surrounding the entire burning area with ditches that are 0.7 to 0.9 m (2–3 ft) wide and that reach down to the mineral soil or groundwater; using powerful foam agents to extinguish flammable liquids; spraying water on the walls of tanks and other metal structures until they have cooled completely

3

4

Wildland Fire Suppression Tactics Reference Guide, National Wildfire Coordinating Group, USA, 1996

This manual from the 1990s shows how many of the most effective principles and tactics developed in the earlier part of the 20th century remained largely unchanged. Stopping the spread of a wildfire by extinguishing it with shovels and

❶ Direct attack is made directly on the fire's edge or perimeter

❷ Parallel attack is made by constructing a fire line [a gap in the vegetation] parallel to, but further from, the fire edge than in a direct attack

❸ Indirect attack is accomplished by building a fire line some distance from the fire edge and back firing the unburnt fuel between the fire line and the fire edge

❹ Hot spotting can be used to cool hot portions of a fire... Hot spotting can be accomplished by building temporary check lines or applying dirt or water

❺ Full containment of the wildfire before it gets to the building(s) is possible... cut off the fire before it reaches the buildings

❻ You may be able to modify or diminish the fire as it hits, but the fire may move past the structure before you can establish control

2. Natural Disaster

'hot spotting' tactics were still the order of the day. The most striking addition here is that of specialized, rugged and agile all-terrain vehicles, with which firefighters could transport people and heavy equipment to key positions, hoping to outpace the flames. Conscious of the potential need for a rapid escape, the manual advises that any vehicles used in firefighting should be left unlocked, with their keys in the ignition, facing away from the fire.

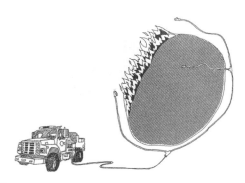

7 A stationary attack is the use of a simple or progressive hose lay from a parked fire engine

8 Mobile attack. The engine is driven along the fire's edge while a nozzle operator applies water parallel to the fire and at the base of the flame

9 Two engines can be used in tandem with a mobile attack

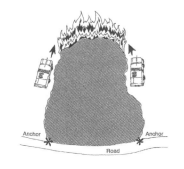

10 A pincer attack is when a fire is attacked from opposite directions by two or more engines

11 The inside-out tactic is a direct attack on the head or flanks of a fire from within the fire perimeter

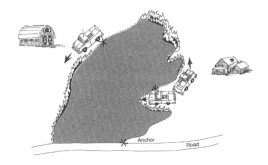

12 The envelopment tactic involves striking key or critical segments or structures around the fire area at approximately the same time

Survive in the Wild

Wilderness survival manuals are most often prepared for those venturing into inhospitable surroundings, and they are intended to be studied by those who put themselves in dangerous scenarios: explorers and adventurers, soldiers, sailors and air crews. However, many of the same skills are also learned by 'civilians', and can be incredibly useful when faced with major disasters. Many of us have an innate fascination with learning survival skills; they can offer ordinary people excitement or reassurance, as well as a chance to escape from the modern world and imagine getting by on our wits alone. Wilderness survival enthusiasts range from TV viewers who experience survival vicariously through personalities such as Bear Grylls, to the millions of Scouts who learn to make campfires and emergency shelters, to the 'preppers' who stockpile food and plan evacuation routes for a disaster that may never come. In extreme circumstances, though, survival techniques can mean the difference between life and death.

When faced with a natural disaster or an emergency situation, a little knowledge can go a long way: as one official survival manual puts it: 'The best time to start learning what to do is before the event.'

According to a UK military survival guide from 1953, there are two vital components to surviving under extreme conditions: the human instinct for self-preservation and an adequate level of training. To this end, most armed forces equip their recruits with wilderness training to prepare them to be self-reliant in combat situations. First aid has been shown to be the best way of avoiding death from injury in battle, and completing a course in the subject has been a requirement of basic training in most modern military forces since the World War II. With home comforts in short supply on the battlefield, most initial military training also includes mandatory survival and fieldcraft classes, which train troops on how to navigate, live and survive in the field. These basic techniques are supplemented by specialist

① Scouts cook over a fire as part of their training at a camp in wartime London, 1943.
② US Scouts listen to their scoutmaster as they learn to whittle wood in the 1950s.
③ Scottish Scouts work together to strike camp at the second World Scout Jamboree in Denmark, 1924.
④ A local skunk provides a true taste of the outdoors for US Scouts at Lake Arrowhead in California.

①

②

③

④

knowledge, depending on the environment into which forces are being sent. This is reflected in the varied range of survival skills training materials distributed to those going into various parts of the world.

Air crews flying over polar regions, for example, are given Arctic survival skills training. This includes how to select a plot to build a shelter; navigating by the stars; constructing and fuelling campfires; gathering food and hunting; and obtaining fresh water. It also describes how to spot and prevent injury from frostbite, hypothermia and carbon monoxide poisoning (from cooking). In addition to the universal need for food and shelter, jungle survival requires quite a different set of skills. These include knowing how to steer clear of mosquitos, snakes and big game; travelling through the undergrowth; building river rafts; and combatting the effects of heat, malaria, dysentery and typhus.

Outside of the military, wilderness survival is learnt and practised by many people for the simple pleasure of building self-reliance and self-confidence. Millions have gained a grounding in survival training thanks to the global Boy Scout and Girl Guide movements. Founded by Lord Baden-Powell on his return to England from the Boer War at the turn of the 20th century, the movements were rooted in the older tradition of military scouting and drew inspiration from American Indian woodcraft. Scouting encourages children to learn essential survival techniques, such as camping, cooking, tracking and first aid, and it provides a basic education in how to cope in the outdoors.

Since the 1990s, a raft of survival-themed television programmes, including *Alone*, *Survivor* and *Man vs Wild*, have gained popularity, making celebrities of survivalists such as Bear Grylls, Les Stroud and Ray Mears. They have also encouraged more adults to take an interest in the subject, leading to the creation of woodcraft training courses and schools. Alongside this trend, the same techniques have become increasingly popular among communities of 'preppers': survivalists who practise a lifestyle built around ensuring complete self-reliance in the event of a war or major disaster.

⑤ ⑥ The covers of *Arctic Survival* and *Jungle Survival*, two life-saving manuals issued to UK airmen in the early 1950s.

Jungle Survival, Air Ministry, UK, 1950

The term 'jungle' covers a wide range of environments, from tropical rainforests to arid, overgrown thickets. The common thread is that vegetation in jungle regions is sufficiently dense that it makes human progress difficult and slow.

Survival tips

❶ If you wish to leave your campsite and later return to it, mark your trail. Blaze trees to show white wood as you proceed

❷ In the lowlands, trees with split roots will indicate swampy and perhaps tidal ground. Avoid all swamps, particularly mangrove swamps

❸ Build a rain trap from large leaves, with the framework made from bamboo or branches

❹ An ideal campsite is: close to water and food; solid ground free from mud; free from dead and decaying vegetation and insects; free from overhanging branches and coconuts; naturally protected from weather and animal life

Making a fire

❶ Rub two pieces of wood together. Note: in 80 per cent humidity, dead wood is 16 per cent water and will not burn

❷ Bow and drill method of making a fire: Draw the bow backwards and forwards causing the drill to spin in its hole... once smoke has been seen to come from the hole in the block, a spark should be found large enough to start a fire

❸ Producing a spark from two stones or flints is all very well, but in practice it will not make fire in the hands of the inexperienced

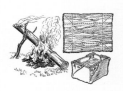

❹ Finding a container in which to boil the water... should not cause any difficulty... as a selection of bamboo will no doubt be found

Air crews sent over such areas were equipped with jungle survival manuals. The UK Air Ministry manual recommends not baling out over a jungle, as not only would you likely sustain injury, but 'you may even find yourself dangling twixt heaven and earth'.

It provides informed advice on the dangers of jungle life: rather than tigers and snakes, it suggests the key hazards are panic, heat, sickness and poisoning. It also provides tips, illustrated here, on choosing a campsite, and making fire, transport and shelter.

Making a log raft

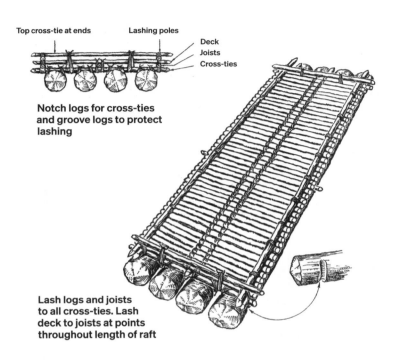

Top cross-tie at ends   Lashing poles

Deck
Joists
Cross-ties

Notch logs for cross-ties and groove logs to protect lashing

Lash logs and joists to all cross-ties. Lash deck to joists at points throughout length of raft

❶ For crossing streams and rivers, make a raft of bamboo or some other light wood. Palm logs and jungle hardwoods do not float. If anyone has to swim across a river, throw stones in the stream and splash about to scare off crocodiles

Making a palm bed and shelter

❶ Make yourself a bed, either by using the parachute canopy you brought with you or by collecting twigs and small branches from trees. Cover a cleared area of ground with branches and then add a further covering of leaves. This will ensure you have a good night's rest, and will also insulate against ground chill and dampness

Dangerous wildlife

1. Bodylouse
2. Sandfly
3. Mosquito
4. Krait
5. Saw-scaled viper
6. Scorpion
7. Centipede
8. Cobra
9. Leeches
10. King cobra
11. Ants
12. Russell's viper
13. Hornet's nest
14. Python

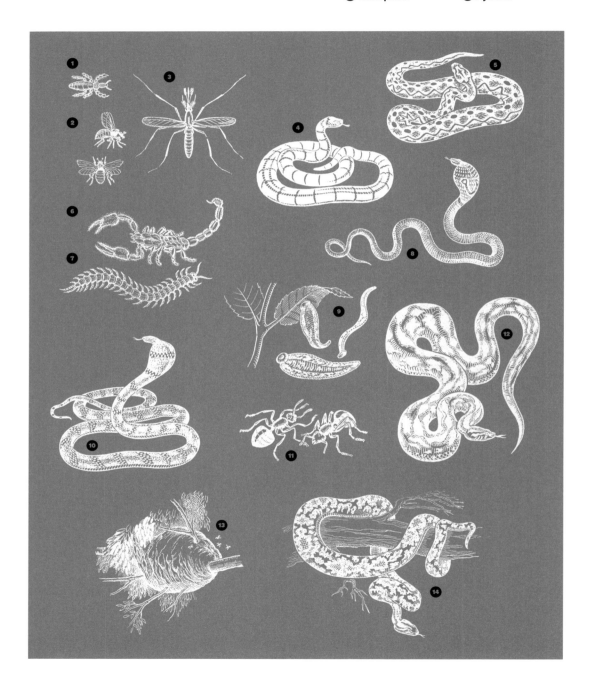

Edible plants, insects and shellfish

1. Sweet potatoes
2. Taro
3. Tapioca
4. Breadfruit
5. Castor oil bean
6. Coconuts
7. Water lilies
8. Bamboo
9. Beetle grubs
10. Grasshoppers
11. Termites
12. Crickets
13. Snails
14. Clams
15. Mussels
16. Limpets
17. Chitons
18. Sea cucumbers
19. Sea urchins
20. Star fish
21. Scallops

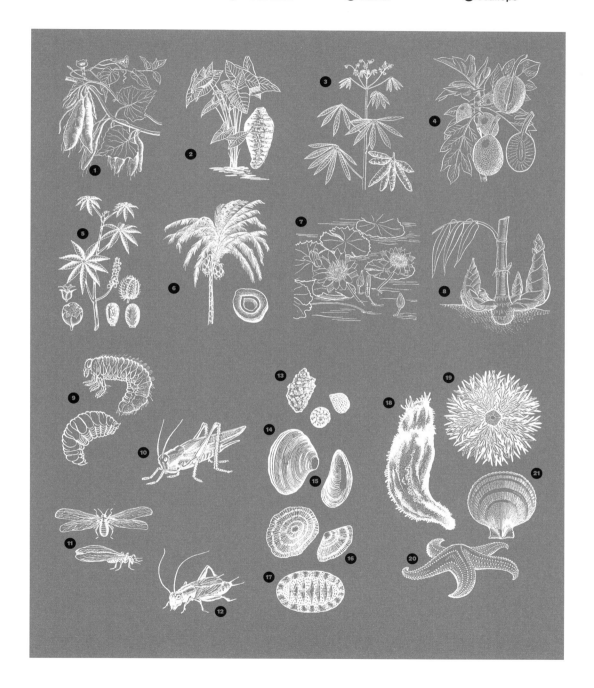

Arctic Survival, Air Ministry, UK, 1953

Temperatures in the Arctic can fall to -40°C (-40°F), and in some places the average summer temperature rarely goes above 10°C (50°F). This combined with the lack of direct sunlight means there is very little vegetation. In this bleak and barren climate, hundreds of miles

Types of shelter

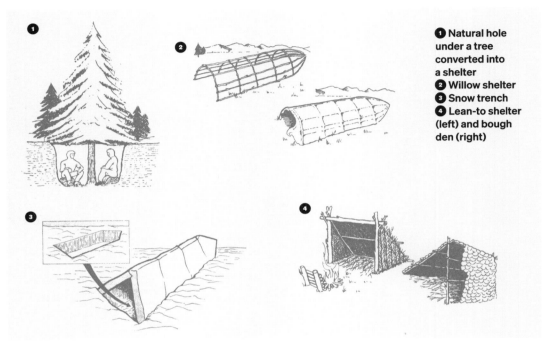

1 Natural hole under a tree converted into a shelter
2 Willow shelter
3 Snow trench
4 Lean-to shelter (left) and bough den (right)

Frostbite

Frostbite appears as a small patch of white or cream-coloured frozen skin, which is firm to the touch and feels stiff. Frostbite can be felt by pulling faces and moving the skin on the face and forehead

Snow blindness

Snow blindness is a temporary form of blindness caused by the high intensity and concentration of the sun's rays, both direct and indirect, reflected from snow-covered ground or ice and ice crystals in the clouds. If, for some reason, you do not have goggles, some kind of eye protection can be made from wood, bark, cloth or paper. Do not use metal

from civilization, it pays to know how to survive. UK airmen flying over the region were issued with a booklet containing detailed survival instructions. The manual from 1953 includes information on how to build shelters using trees, snow blocks or even the wing of your downed aircraft. It also details the risks of cold weather, such as frostbite, snow blindness and poor hygiene, since taking a bath is out of the question in freezing conditions. Additionally, the manual shows how to construct fish traps, gather molluscs for food and navigate by the stars.

Orientation: stars

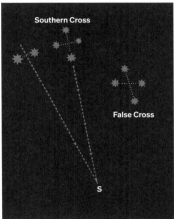

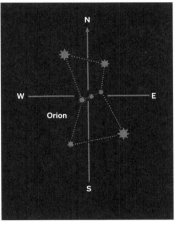

1 In the Northern Hemisphere, true north can be ascertained from the constellation of the Great Bear, which points to Polaris (North Star), the star over the North Pole

2 In the Southern Hemisphere, the Southern Cross indicates the direction south

3 Other constellations, such as Orion, rise in the east and set in the west, moving to the south of you when you are north of the equator and vice versa

Trail blazing

Blaze your trail. If the entire survival party is going to walk out, or if a small group is setting out to get help, messages stating the intended route should be left at the base camp. In the Arctic, communication is very slow, and the more signs of your presence along the trail the greater your chance of being found. Mark your trail clearly. Strange trails are nearly always followed by trappers and native people

	Cut branches	Rock placement	Tree marks	Stone arrows
Straight ahead				
Turn right				
Turn left				

US Air Force Survival School, Department of the Air Force, USA, 1985

This manual for US air crews took into account the psychological well-being of downed airmen and the physical conditions they might encounter. It stated that survival would be unlikely if they were not mentally prepared and gave examples of what they might expect.

Psychological conditions

1 Pain is uncomfortable but is not, in itself, harmful or dangerous **2** Thirst and dehydration are among the most critical problems facing survivors **3** Cold is a serious threat because even in mild degrees it lowers efficiency **4** Just as numbness is the principle symptom of cold, weakness is the principle symptom of heat **5** Hunger and semi-starvation are more commonly experienced among survivors than thirst and dehydration **6** Frustration occurs when one's efforts are stopped, either by obstacles blocking progress towards a goal or by not having a realistic goal **7** As a survivor, depression is the greatest psychological problem that has to be conquered **8** In a survival episode, a survivor must continually cope with fatigue **9** Fear can save a life, or it can cost one **10** The captive environment is the prime area where a survivor may experience feelings

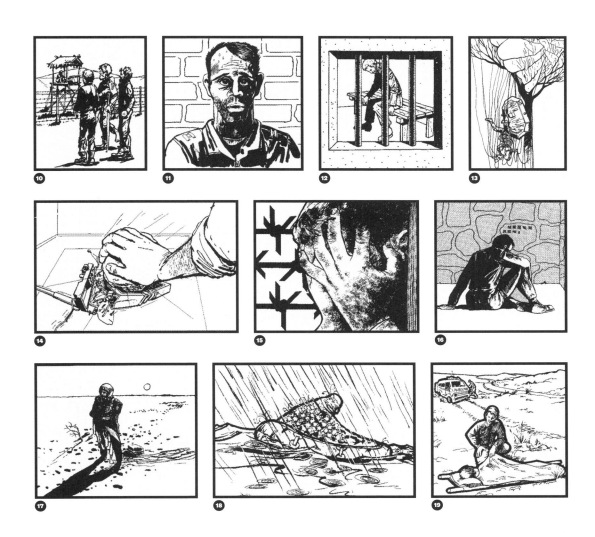

of dependency ⑪ Anxiety... can be felt when changes occur that affect an individual's safety, plan or method of living ⑫ Survivors soon begin to miss daily interactions with other people ⑬ In the face of danger, a person may panic or freeze, and cease to function in an organized manner ⑭ Anger is a strong feeling of displeasure and belligerence aroused by a real or supposed wrong ⑮ Loneliness can be very debilitating during a survival episode ⑯ Boredom and fatigue are related and are frequently confused ⑰ Hopelessness stems from negative feelings: regardless of actions taken, success seems impossible ⑱ The effects of sleep loss are closely related to those of fatigue ⑲ The will to survive is the desire to live despite seemingly insurmountable mental and/or physical obstacles

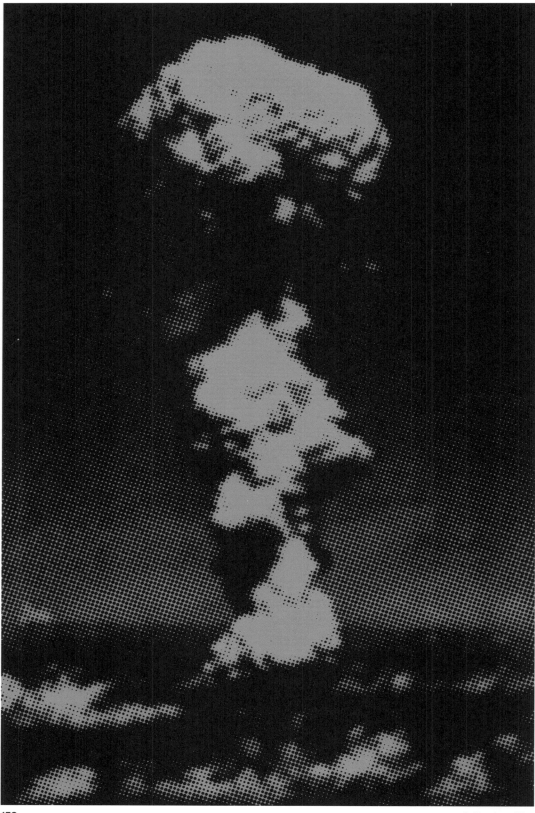

Nuclear War

Preparation 160
Shelter 174
Blast and Fallout 186

THREE PLANS FOR SURVIVAL IN A NUCLEAR ATTACK

Protect and Survive[*]
Preparing for Nuclear War

* 'Protect and Survive' was a public information campaign produced by the UK government. It included several films and a pamphlet. The pamphlet initially had a very limited release, sent only to local authorities. However, after content was leaked in *The Times*, the government was forced to issue it to the public in May 1980.

① *Live: Three Plans for Survival in a Nuclear Attack*, USA, 1960. Civil defence against nuclear attack captured the public imagination in the early 1960s. The stylized illustration on the cover imitates *Life* magazine, and shows families sheltering from deadly radioactive fallout.

In previous chapters, we considered pandemics and natural disasters, which – while horrifying – are catastrophes we can at least comprehend. Nuclear war is different. How do you prepare the public for something that is not only horrific, but also virtually inconceivable: a disaster created by weapons of unimaginable power, the use of which only a tiny fraction of humanity has ever experienced?

However unthinkable nuclear war might be, governments spent the Atomic Age trying to reassure people that there were realistic, practical measures that they could take to ensure their survival. Many countries created programmes of 'civil defence', with civilian volunteers taking on roles in which they would prepare the public ahead of nuclear attack, and help deal with the aftermath. Alongside this, governments produced printed materials to advise the public on what they should expect – and how to act – when it happened.

In the late 1940s, with World War II recently ended, the Cold War was just dawning. Early materials on nuclear attack from this period

Introduction

were optimistic in a way that seems rather jarring today. One UK public information pamphlet summed up the prevailing line of thought, saying: 'Civil defence can beat atomic bombs.' This misplaced confidence dissipated during the 1950s, a decade that saw the development of a new kind of nuclear weapon: the hydrogen or H-bomb. The obvious and chilling power of nuclear weapons meant governments could not continue to mask the truth about nuclear attack; groundless optimism was replaced by the idea that things would be bad, but you stood a better chance of survival if you were well-informed.

Depictions of nuclear attack became starker, but also sought to educate. They described the effects of a nuclear bomb, showed how to fortify your home against deadly fallout and attempted to reassure people by explaining the investments being made in civil defence services. Then, in 1961, the Soviet Union tested the largest nuclear bomb ever created: the Tsar Bomba. At 50 megatons, it packed a terrifying punch more than 3,000 times that of the weapon dropped on Hiroshima just 16 years earlier. The following year, the Cuban Missile Crisis saw the world brought to the brink of nuclear annihilation for the first time. Teetering on the edge of conflict, governments changed the tone and style of official advice to their panicked citizens, simplifying instructions and focusing on practical measures householders could take.

② This Hungarian poster from the 1960s says that it is patriotic to carry out civil defence duties.

③ Civil defence is promoted as a common cause: 'The most important task of civil defence is to protect human life and property.'

④ This poster advises Hungarians to be prepared to implement civil defence practices.

②

③

④

Nuclear advice was published on both sides of the Cold War. While there were some universal themes – shelter, survival, fallout – approaches to the presentation of the guidance split along ideological lines. Advice in Western countries focused on how individuals and families could protect themselves, depicting people making their own homes safe against nuclear attack, and creating single-family fallout shelters. Conversely, materials from the Eastern bloc and from China were far more likely to show people working together outdoors, in shared communal shelters, or making provisions for their communities – often aided by state actors, such as civil defence forces, hospital staff or soldiers.

By the 1970s and 1980s, it began to become obvious that there would be no winners in a nuclear war. The principle of mutually assured destruction, or MAD, emerged; it held that neither side would launch an attack, because there were now enough weapons on both sides to destroy the world several times over. New discoveries found that the electromagnetic pulse (EMP) released by an air-burst nuclear weapon could knock out electronic devices for miles, including car starters, radios and telephone networks. Together with the influence of the anti-nuclear protest movement, concepts such as MAD and EMP played on the public imagination. They deepened the feeling of widespread hopelessness and underlined the ridiculous nature of the nuclear threat.

⑤ Australia's official guide to nuclear attack was published in 1984. It was based on UK guides from the 1950s. ⑥ The UK government's infamous *Protect and Survive* manual was part of a wider public information campaign on nuclear war.

In the West, official government advice was no longer received in an interested or even passive way, instead being openly criticized and mocked. Thus, by the end of the Cold War in 1991, governments had already stepped back from producing civil defence materials.

It is remarkable today to see how much information governments produced on protecting individuals, families and communities against nuclear attack – and it is remarkably fortunate that it was never needed.

⑤

⑥

Preparation

In most countries, domestic preparations for nuclear attack were assigned to government-sponsored civil defence services. These organizations would train men in specialisms such as rescue from buildings, treating casualties, firefighting and monitoring radiation. Women would be encouraged to participate in welfare services, concentrating on evacuating the vulnerable and aiding the homeless, setting up rest centres and running emergency kitchens. While these organizations could ostensibly be called upon to assist in any disaster, their primary role was to prepare for nuclear attack.

In the United States, the civil defence organization was the community's front line against nuclear attack, and it proudly sported the 'CD' brand – a blue triangle within an orange circle – on much of its literature. The international symbol for civil defence was also used in Canada and across much of Europe. By the 1950s, France, Sweden, Norway, the Netherlands, West Germany and Denmark all had their own fully fledged civil defence services – as did neutral countries such as Switzerland and Ireland. In the United Kingdom, the Civil Defence Corps took on the community role, while another organization, the Royal Observer Corps, was assigned the duty of monitoring the skies for nuclear attack.

However, few countries in the West took civil defence quite as seriously as the United States. There, preparing for nuclear attack invaded every part of life. Car radios were marked with the correct frequency to tune into for updates, schools and colleges practised emergency drills and the civil defence symbol even appeared on Mister Softee ice cream vans, which carried a generator, food, water, a loudspeaker and floodlights. Each truck was ready to play a welfare role after an atomic attack.

Civil defence services existed in most communist and socialist countries, too, with particularly well-developed forces in the Soviet Union, Czechoslovakia, Hungary and East Germany. The Soviet Union, the

①

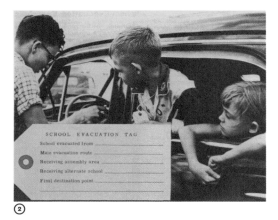

②

③

① This fallout shelter was built above ground for demonstration purposes in 1952. Normally, entry would be through the shaft at the top. ② Children are given tags during the evacuation of a school in Mobile, Alabama, as part of a dummy run ahead of nuclear attack. ③ Vehicles wait in line to leave Mobile as part of the practice evacuation, dubbed 'Operation Kids', in 1956.

④ A family shows that they are prepared for nuclear war in Nevada, 1955. Families were advised to stockpile enough nonperishable foods to stay alive in their fallout room or shelter for several weeks. ⑤ Making his first appearance in 1952, instructional cartoon character Bert the Turtle taught US children to find shelter, and – infamously – to 'Duck and Cover'. ⑥ School children practicing an atom bomb drill in Cleveland, Ohio, 1951. ⑦ US schoolchildren became well-versed in the 'duck and cover' method of personal protection thanks to regular atomic attack drills, such as this one in Florida, 1962.

④

⑤

⑥

3. Nuclear War

other great nuclear superpower, made civil defence education part of public life. Like their US counterparts, Soviet schoolchildren took part in regular mandatory civil defence drills, learning how to stay calm and take action should a nuclear strike be launched.

Through their civil defence services, governments issued advice to the public in the form of guidebooks, pamphlets and posters. In 1959, the US Department of Defence issued *Ten for Survival*, a simple illustrated guide showing how to construct a fallout shelter and prepare it for your family ahead of disaster. 1961 saw the Canadian government create its *Blueprint for Survival* series, while the Dutch government distributed *Hints for Protecting your Family and Yourself* (*Wenken voor de bescherming van uw gezin en uzelf*) to every home. The Danes published *If War Should Come* (*Hvis krigen kommer*) in 1962, and the UK government issued *Advising the Householder on Protection Against Nuclear Attack* in 1963. France followed with *Know to Live* (*Savoir pour vivre*) in 1965. All these booklets contained a common set of topics: a primer on what to expect from a nuclear explosion; building and equipping your fallout shelter; what different sirens mean; and what you and your family should do before, during and after attack.

⑦

Air raid defence posters, Red Cross, Japan, 1938

Japanese homes came under air attack in 1938 as the country fought in the Second Sino-Japanese War. These posters were created to advise citizens on preparing their homes and taking shelter when ordered to do so during an air raid.

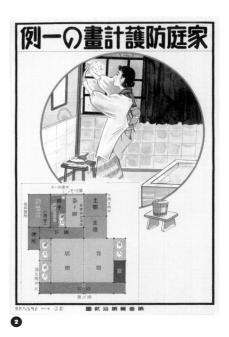

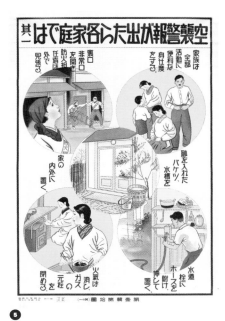

❺

❻

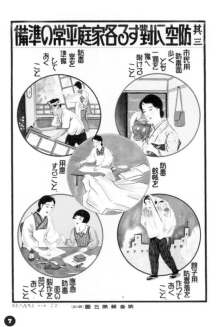

❼

❽

Home Protection Exercises, Federal Civil Defence Administration, USA, 1953

Like many civil defence guides from this period, this manual claims to offer tips that would be useful in any disaster, while clearly having nuclear attack in mind. To that end, alongside tips on preparing your fallout shelter and recognizing the attack

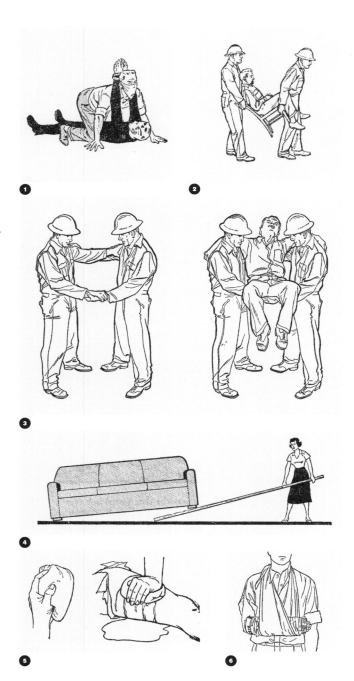

❶ To find a missing member of the family, rescuers should begin at the bottom of the house and work upwards. If the victim is unconscious when found, put them on the floor unless their injuries prevent it. If they must be moved, carefully turn the victim on their back and tie their wrists together with a handkerchief or other article of clothing. By kneeling astride the victim and putting your head between the tied wrists, you can then crawl forward, dragging the victim behind you ❷ A chair may be used as a stretcher in an emergency. Raise the victim to sitting position and lift them gently into the chair, supporting their knees and back. One rescuer can then carry the chair by its front legs, the other by its back legs ❸ Two rescuers can make a seat on which to carry a conscious victim. Each rescuer steadies the victim with an arm around their back. Then each rescuer slides his other arm under the victim's thighs and clasps the other's wrist. One pair of arms makes a seat rest, the other pair a back rest. Both rescuers then rise slowly in unison, lifting the victim from the ground ❹ Some kind of lever is useful for lifting wreckage or heavy debris off a victim. Your home contains many things that could be used as levers: bed slats, spare lengths of pipe, a pick or shovel or even an ironing board. When using a lever to raise wreckage from a victim, you should prop up the object to keep it from falling back on them ❺ For serious bleeding, first get the victim to lie down and remain quiet. Try to stop the bleeding by pressing a cloth pad directly on the wound itself. Towels, sheets or anything else at hand can be used for emergency pads ❻ If it is absolutely necessary to move a victim with a broken bone, first put a splint on the fracture. A splint is a piece of wood secured to the victim so that the ends of the broken bone cannot move

warning sirens, it gives practical advice on caring for your nearest and dearest in an emergency situation. This includes step-by-step instructions on fighting fires within the home, helping trapped people, finding safe food and water, and dealing with injuries. The illustrations presented here show how to rescue and care for family members injured in the home during a disaster. Had that catastrophe been an atomic bomb, the scenes depict a rather optimistic view of post-attack life.

❼ Every homemaker should know how to change bed linen with a patient in bed. Clean sheets should be available. A blanket or robe should be used to cover the patient while the linen is being changed. Follow the pictures; they show you how to change the bed linen

❽ When a patient has been confined to bed for any length of time, it is essential that alcohol back rubs be given. The alcohol rub helps protect the skin, aids blood circulation and prevents bed sores

❾ When bathing a patient, a towel should be placed under the portion of the body being washed. Cover the patient with a bath blanket. Wash the patient's face, neck and ears first. Rinse and dry well. Next, wash shoulders, armpits, arms and hands. Rinse and dry well. Put the towel across the patient's chest. Fold a bath blanket down to the patient's belly. Raise the towel and wash the chest. Pay special attention to the skin, especially on the back, shoulders, heels, elbows and under the breasts of women patients. After rinsing, dry thoroughly

❼

❽

❾

Advising the Householder, Home Office, UK, 1963

This guide offers practical advice on constructing a shelter to protect yourself from nuclear threat, providing you have plenty of sandbags and heavy furniture. It also offers tips on avoiding the worst of the nuclear blast if you are caught outdoors.

Protective measures

1 If you live in a house, choose a room on the ground floor with as little outside wall as possible **2** Rooms in flats on the middle floors would give the best protection **3** If you live in a bungalow or single-storey prefabricated house, these dwellings give little protection **4** Remove [window] frames and put boards, planks or doors across outer and inner sills as shutters **5** Or remove the frames and brick up the openings **6** Put sandbags or earth-filled containers outside the windows. If you cannot do this, block the windows from inside with bookcases, chests of drawers or other large furniture packed tightly with earth, books or other heavy material

Shelter core

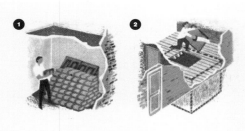

1 Better protection could be obtained by constructing a shelter core. This is a smaller, thick-walled shelter, built preferably inside the fallout room itself, in which to spend the first critical hours when radiation from fallout would be most dangerous. The core could take various forms: for example, a lean-to of wood, sandbagged over and resting against an inner wall **2** An underfloor trench **3** A cupboard under the stairs, sandbagged on the stairs and along the outside of the cupboard **4** If it is impossible for you to prepare an indoor fallout shelter, a trench dug outside your home would provide good protection

Warnings

	SOUND	MEANING
	Siren (rising and falling note)	Imminent danger of attack
	Siren (interrupted note of steady pitch) or church bells	Fallout expected in an hour
	Maroon, gong or whistle sounding a Morse D – dash dot dot	Imminent danger of fallout

❶ If there has already been a red warning, do not expose yourself needlessly to the risk of air attack. The grey warning does not mean that another attack could not come ❷ In open country, make for any cover or, failing that, lie down in a ditch or depression in the ground, covering the exposed skin of the face and hands ❸ At home, go immediately to your fallout room ❹ The warning system aims to give notice of the threat of air attack and also of fallout

What to do if it happens

❶ If you have been caught out of doors, take off your outer garments and leave them outside the fallout room; brush your remaining clothes and wash exposed parts of the body before going to the shelter. This would help to get rid of any fallout dust you may have picked up outside ❷ Give shelter to anyone caught without protection near your home ❸ If an explosion comes without warning, the first you would know of it would be a blinding flash of heat and light lasting about 20 seconds ❹ Outdoors, take cover against the heat flash by flinging yourself down instantly wherever you are ❺ At home, move instantly away from windows or open doorways and get behind anything solid... remain under the best available cover until the blast wave is over. Then put out fires

DO NOT LOOK AT THE FLASH

Civil Defence (Zivilschutzfibel), Federal Office for the Civil Protection of Bad Godesberg, West Germany, 1964

On the front lines of European nuclear tension, civil defence was serious business. Like many of its kind, this booklet covers a plethora of potential disasters, but its focus is on preparing the population for nuclear attack.

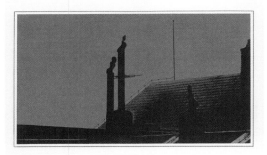

①

②

③

④

⑤

⑥

⑦

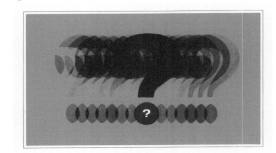

⑧

Zivilshutzfibel contains advice on multiple different aspects of nuclear war survival, including information on the flash itself ①, biological and chemical weapons ②, the importance of staying at home ③ and of safety bunkers ④, nuclear weapons ⑤ ⑦, the opinions of scientists ⑥, how to help yourself and others in an attack ⑧ ⑨ ⑩, fire safety ⑪, the contents of your evacuation bag ⑫, where to find help ⑬, essential medical supplies ⑭, what the state is doing ⑮ and advised food and water provisions ⑯.

⑨

⑩

⑪

⑫

⑬

⑭

⑮

⑯

Preparation

What to Do... (Co dělat...),
Federal Ministry of the Interior,
Czechoslovakia, 1972

This Z-fold pamphlet was produced by the
Czechoslovak Socialist Republic Federal Ministry
of the Interior with the army, and designed by Václav
Deyl. Its includes how the alarm will be sounded in
different types of attack ②, evacuation supplies ③,

⑥ ⑤ ④

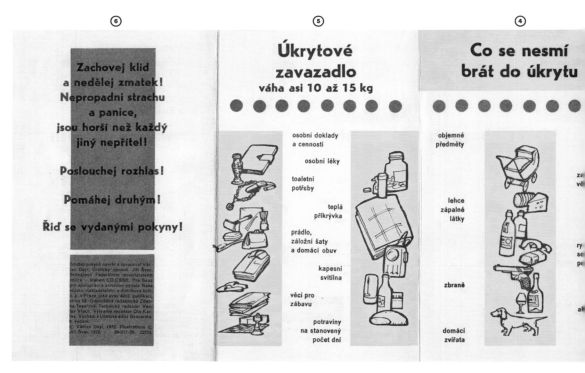

Zachovej klid
a nedělej zmatek!
Nepropadni strachu
a panice,
jsou horší než každý
jiný nepřítel!

Poslouchej rozhlas!

Pomáhej druhým!

Řiď se vydanými pokyny!

Úkrytové zavazadlo
váha asi 10 až 15 kg

osobní doklady
a cennosti

osobní léky

toaletní
potřeby

teplá
přikrývka

prádlo,
záložní šaty
a domácí obuv

kapesní
svítilna

věci pro
zábavu

potraviny
na stanovený
počet dní

Co se nesmí brát do úkrytu

objemné
předměty

lehce
zápalné
látky

zbraně

domácí
zvířata

Vyhlašování
Vyhláška FMV
Rozhlas
a televize
Denní tisk

Situace ohrožení

řídit se vyhláškou
zvýšit ostražitost
odebrat prostředky
IPCHO
provést zatemnění
opatřit a zabalit
potraviny
zúčastnit se stavby
a úpravy úkrytů
připravit v bytech
zásobu vody
připravit zavazadlo
a oděv do úkrytu
poslouchat sdělovací
prostředky
znát domovní uzávěry
ve městech vyjmout
vnitřní okna
(připravit se
na evakuaci tam,
kde se s ní počítá)

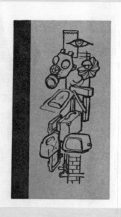

Vyhlašování
Sirény
Parní píšťaly
Místní rozhlas

Vzdušný poplach

upozornit sousedy

uhasit ohniště

vypnout spotřebiče

uzavřít plyn
v bytě i v domě

vypnout v bytě
elektřinu

vzít prostředky
individuální proti-
chemické ochrany

pomoci nemocným
a starým

vzít úkrytové zavazadlo

odejít do úkrytu

Vyhlašování
Vyhláška
Rozhlas
Televize
Místní rozhlas

Evakuace

upozornit sousedy

uhasit ohniště

vypnout spotřebiče
a elektřinu

uzavřít vnější okna

uzavřít domovní uzávěry
plynu a vody

obléknout se na cestu

vzít si prostředky
IPCHO a osob. doklady

vzít si evakuační
zavazadlo

vzít si stravu
na 2 až 3 dny

uzamknout byt

odejít do evakuačního
střediska a řídit se po-
kyny regulační služby

⑫ ⑪ ⑩

which supplies should ⑤ and should not ④ be taken into a shelter, the instruction to 'keep calm and do not cause panic! Do not succumb to fear and panic; they are worse than any other enemy! Listen to the radio! Help others! Follow issued instructions!' ⑥,

general civil defence instructions ⑫ and specific instructions for different alerts: the alert for chemical attack ⑦, the alert for radiation ⑧, the alert for radiation and chemical attack ⑨, the alert for evacuation ⑩ and air alarm ⑪.

③   ②   ①

...akuační zavazadlo

do 50 kg pro dospělé
do 25 kg pro děti

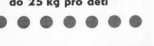

osobní doklady
a cennosti

osobní léky
a obvazy

základní
potraviny
na 2 až 3 dny
čaj (voda)

předměty
osobní hygieny

předměty
denní potřeby

kapesní svítilna,
svíčka, zápalky

domácí obuv

přikrývka
(spací pytel)

prádlo
a záložní
oděv, obuv
a nepromokavý
plášť

Konec poplachu

vzdušného
sirény, parní píšťaly

radiačního
místní rozhlas,
telefon, spojky

chemického
místní rozhlas,
telefon, spojky

Co dělat
za
situací
a signálů
civilní
obrany

...hlašování
**Místními
rozhlašovacími
prostředky**

...diační
...chemické nebezpečí

...e mimo
...v (praco-
...ihned se

...it potraviny
...hranu proti
...ření

...čit úpravu
...ení pro ukry-
...ryty, úkrytové
...ranné
...ory)

...vit se na
...d do úkrytů
...obyt
...ranné
...ytové
...oře)

**Vyhlašování
Zvony
Místní rozhlas**

Radiační
poplach

- nasadit prostředky individuální protichemické ochrany do ochranné polohy
- uhasit ohniště, vypnout plynové a elektrické spotřebiče
- vzit úkrytové zavazadlo a odejit do úkrytu (úkryto-

ÚKRYT 50 m → K

vé nebo ochranné prostory) a podrobit se režimu stanovenému pro pobyt v úkrytu v zamořeném prostoru

**Vyhlašování
Rozhlašovacími
prostředky:
„Pozor: Chemický
poplach!" Údery
na kov. předměty**

Chemický poplach

ihned nasadit
prostředky
individuální
protichemické
ochrany do
ochranné polohy

uhasit ohniště,
vypnout plynové
a elektrické
spotřebiče

vzit připravenou
zásobu potravin

vzit úkrytové za-
vazadlo a odejit
do úkrytu

úkryty
chráni před
BOL jen tehdy,
maji-li filtro-

ÚKRYT K

ventilační zařízení v chodu; není-li tomu tak, nutno používat prostředky protichemické ochrany jednotlivce

⑨   ⑧   ⑦

Shelter

Public information booklets emphasized shelter as the main form of protection from nuclear attack. 'The best protection against fallout radiation is a fallout shelter,' said the US government's *Ten for Survival*. 'Everyone should have one.' Typically, this shelter would take the form of a reinforced and sealed-off fallout room, somewhere close to the middle of a building or in a basement. UK pamphlets described this as an 'inner core or refuge'. Another option was to construct an outdoor shelter, either below the ground or covered over with earth, or surrounded with two layers of bricks. The idea here was to offer protection against the deadly effects of radioactive fallout, which could last several weeks. People living in anything other than a traditional house – such as an apartment block – were often simply ignored.

Advice was also given on how to stock your fallout shelter. The UK's *Domestic Nuclear Shelters* guidebook, published in 1981, suggests having enough food and water for two weeks, a portable radio and a plethora of handy items, such as can openers, warm clothing, torches with spare batteries and bulbs, makeshift toilet facilities, a clock and a calendar.

Despite officials' best efforts to educate people on the importance of building their own shelters, the public were not particularly receptive. In 1961, President John F. Kennedy stated that the US Civil Defence programme had been met with 'apathy, indifference and scepticism', and called for more to be done. He encouraged the development of a public fallout shelter programme, and funding was provided for shelters to be created across the country. While these may not have protected against the initial blast, they at least offered people a place to shelter from the fallout afterwards.

On the other side of the Iron Curtain, the Soviet Union also embarked on an ambitious mass shelter scheme, cleverly building subways and metro stations that could withstand nuclear attack. Some European countries, such as Finland, Norway, Sweden and Switzerland, built provision for public shelters into tunnels and government buildings, and mandated that new buildings should include nuclear shelters. The UK made no such preparations to protect the public. During the 1960s, a 'dispersal scheme' was drawn up to evacuate vulnerable people to the countryside, but this plan was abandoned soon afterwards, and individuals were left to fend for themselves – with the help of government guidebooks, of course.

① Emergency drill in Switzerland, 1984. Despite its neutrality, Switzerland had one of the world's leading civil defence programmes, with bunkers built in many public and private buildings. ② A bunker cohabitation exercise in Switzerland, 1984. ③ The early 1980s saw a boom in private bunker sales. This one is being modelled by the Millet family in north London, UK. ④ In 1964, seven students subjected themselves to six days of post-apocalyptic life in a nuclear bunker in Dortmund, Germany. ⑤ Drinking in the massive underground Marieberget bomb shelter in Vasteras, Sweden, May 1962. Swedish bunkers formed part of the fabric of everyday life. This shelter housed public facilities, including a gymnasium and youth centre.

①

②

③

④

⑤

The Family Fallout Shelter, Office of Civil and Defence Mobilization, USA, 1959

Published by the US Federal Government, *The Family Fallout Shelter* contains building plans for five basic fallout shelters, one of which – the basement concrete block shelter – is designed as a do-it-yourself project. The manual warns: 'There are means of protection. But that protection must be provided before, not after, the sirens sound.'

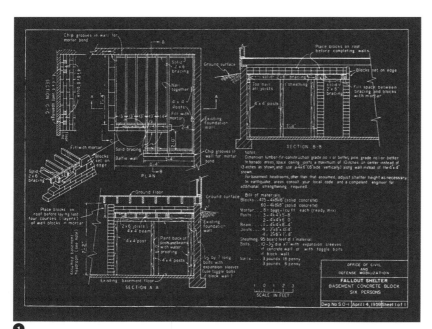

❶

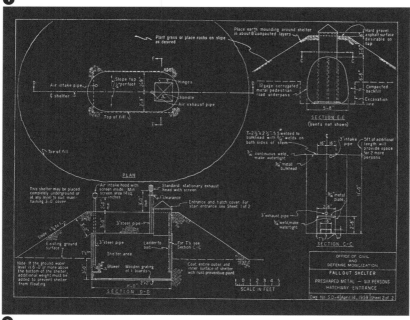

❷

❶ Plan for a basement shelter, using concrete blocks. Accommodates six people **❷** Plan for a fallout shelter using preshaped metal, featuring a hatchway entrance. Accommodates six people

Basement concrete block shelter

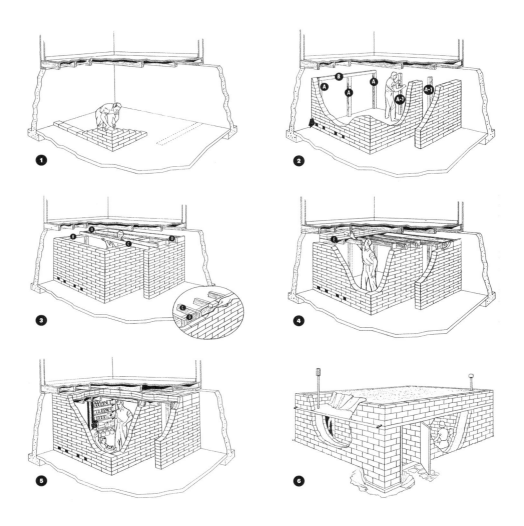

① A row of solid concrete blocks is set in about 10 mm (⅜ in.) of wet mortar along guidelines marked on the basement floor. The corner is built about six blocks high. The remainder of the wall is then built to the same height. The corner is built up once more and the wall again raised to its level ② Ventilation is provided by an open doorway and vents near the floor in one wall. The posts (marked A and A-1) that support the roof beams are fixed to the basement walls with 12-mm (½-in.) anchor bolts. A wall beam (marked B) is put in place against the original wall from one corner post to the other ③ The roof beams (marked C) are installed after the mortar in the block wall has dried (at least one day). One end of each roof beam is nailed to the wall beam (marked B). The roof beams are placed on edge. Wood braces (marked D) hold them in place ④ The first one or two roof boards (marked E) are slipped into place across the roof beams, from outside the shelter. These boards are nailed to the roof beams by reaching up through the open space between the beams (from inside the shelter). Concrete blocks are passed between the beams and put on the boards. The roof blocks are set in two layers and are not mortared together ⑤ When the roof blocks are all in place, the final rows of wall blocks are mortared into position ⑥ The above-ground double-wall shelter is complete

Know to Live (*Savoir pour vivre*), National Service for Civil Protection, France, 1960

Personal hygiene

Portable toilet

Plastic bags for toilet

Toilet paper

Hand flannels

Towels

Wash bowl

Beauty products

Soap

Toothbrush

Razor

Shaving soap

Shaving brush

Razor blades

Toothpaste

Comb

Hairbrush

Essentials

Lime chlorine

Bleach

Calendar

Newspapers

Road map

Bucket pump

Fire extinguisher

Battery-powered radio

Insecticide

Clock

Leisure

Bible

Books

Hobbies

Playing cards

Games

Children's toys

This comprehensive and richly illustrated French civil defence manual covers every aspect of nuclear attack, from building a lean-to shelter to first aid, including what to do with dead bodies. The manual is divided into three sections: fire, first aid and the dangers of radioactivity. constructing a fallout shelter and surviving within it are described within the final section, which includes a checklist of all the essential equipment.

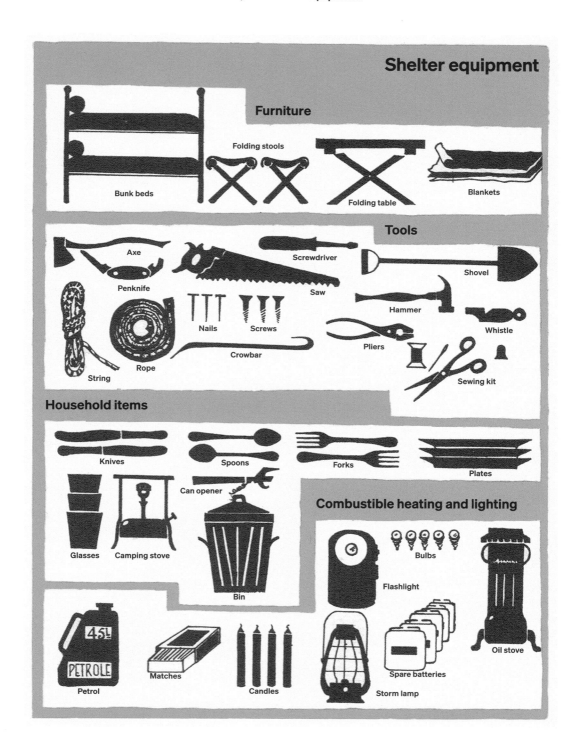

Shelter equipment

Furniture

Folding stools

Bunk beds

Folding table

Blankets

Tools

Axe

Penknife

Screwdriver

Shovel

Saw

Hammer

Nails

Screws

Crowbar

Pliers

Whistle

String

Rope

Sewing kit

Household items

Knives

Spoons

Forks

Plates

Can opener

Glasses

Camping stove

Bin

Combustible heating and lighting

Bulbs

Flashlight

Oil stove

4.5L

PETROLE

Matches

Candles

Spare batteries

Storm lamp

Petrol

Live: Three Plans for Survival in Nuclear Attack, Stanford Research Institute, USA, 1960

This manual was prepared by the Stanford Research Institute, a research centre in Menlo Park, California, which was part of Stanford University. The guide was prepared specifically to advise the institute's staff members and their immediate families on their

Emergency shelter

In general, you will need to be behind something with a mass and weight equivalent to at least 0.9 m (3 ft) of earth to have sufficient protection from radiation levels expected in this area after an attack.

Caves, culverts and sandbagging over a frame such as a table are possible expedients.

More than likely, however, your most accessible and effective shelter would be in the basement of a nearby building.

You should be guided by the numbers on the accompanying illustration, which indicate the extent to which fallout from the ground and rooftops would be reduced.

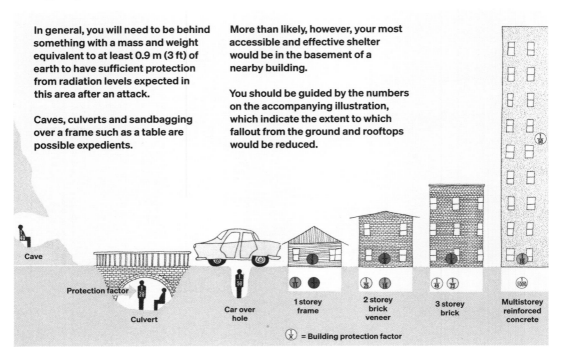

Cave

Protection factor

Culvert

Car over hole

1 storey frame

2 storey brick veneer

3 storey brick

Multistorey reinforced concrete

$\left(\frac{1}{x}\right)$ = Building protection factor

Types of shelter

❶ Above-ground double-wall shelter: no blast protection... Reduction of radiation to $\frac{1}{1000}$ of outside levels... Good for areas where water or rock is close to the surface and an underground shelter is therefore impractical ❷ Basement concrete block shelter: no blast protection... Reduction of radiation to $\frac{1}{200}$ of outside levels... Easy to construct by yourself. Hazardous if house catches fire ❸ Underground reinforced concrete shelter: possibly some blast protection (not yet tested)... Reduction of radiation to $\frac{1}{5000}$ of outside levels ❹ Metal arch shelter: blast protection of 30 psi (verified by Nevada test)... Reduction of radiation to $\frac{1}{500}$ of outside levels

shelter and survival options in case of nuclear attack. The eponymous 'three plans' refer to three potential options for survival: a communal basement shelter, a homemade shelter or evacuation. The booklet provides a variety of options for constructing fallout shelters in order to survive a Soviet atomic strike. Some, such as the above-ground shelter, would only provide shelter from deadly fallout; more robust shelters could also help families survive the initial blast effects.

Method of construction

1 Dig a hole 2.7 m (9 ft) in diameter and 2.7 m (9 ft) deep, for shelter pipe. In that hole, dig another hole 0.6 m (2 ft) in diameter and 1.2 m (4 ft) deep, for storage pipe **2** Place storage pipe in the smaller hole so that top of storage pipe is flush with door. Pour concrete floor, if you are using one, as footing for shelter pipe. Place a tar rope seal on pipe seating. Have a 2.4-m (8-ft) section of 2.4-m (8-ft) diameter concrete pipe delivered in the larger hole. Fill in gap around the outside of shelter pipe with dirt. Cut 2×4s or 2×6s in appropriate lengths and place across top of the shelter pipe **3** Place corrugated entrance pipe in position resting on 2×4s. Support 12-mm (½-in.) reinforcing rods 150 mm (6 in.) on centre, 50 mm (2 in.) above 2×4s and wire at each crossing. Pour 150 mm (6 in.) slab roof concrete over 2×4s **4** Cut hole in 2×4s at bottom of entrance pipe to make shelter entrance. Place sheet of vinyl plastic over slab as water seal. Cover roof with dirt, carefully grading away from shelter to avoid drainage problem. Finish as desired

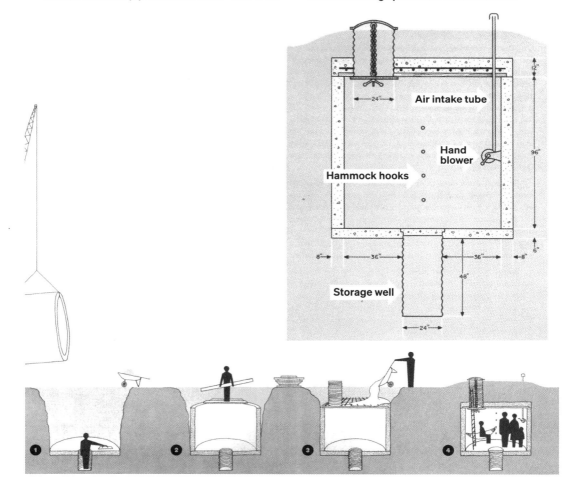

Air intake tube

Hand blower

Hammock hooks

Storage well

Fallout Protection, Office of Civil Defence, USA, 1961

This booklet presents a selection of shelters for homeowners, to suit all budgets and time frames. The options range from an improvised lean-to shelter weighed down with sand, to a back garden prefab tube shelter, complete with air vents.

❶ A model public shelter and community centre **❷** Built-in shelter in new structure **❸** After nuclear attack, a tall apartment or office building, 16 km (10 mi) or more from the explosion, could be one of the safest refuges **❹** This family is building a basement compact shelter from sand-filled concrete blocks. Solid concrete blocks are used for the roof shielding. This type of shelter could also be built of brick or structural tiles **❺** This sand-filled lean-to basement shelter will accommodate three people. The house itself gives partial shielding. Sandbags are used to block the end of the shelter **❻** This backyard plywood shelter can be built partially above ground and mounded over with earth, or it can be built totally below ground level **❼** This prefab backyard shelter for four can be bought for under $150. The price includes the corrugated steel-pipe unit (1.2 m [4 ft] diameter), entry point and air vent pipes **❽** This four-person basement corner shelter is made of curved asbestos-cement sheets, which are covered with sandbags. Materials cost about $125 **❾** If you do not have a basement, you can improvise a shelter by digging a trench next to your house and making a lean-to structure using house doors **❿** This man is improvising a fallout shelter in a basement corner by stacking heavy material on and at the open sides of a sturdy table

❽

❾

❿

Shelter

Domestic Nuclear Shelters, Home Office, UK, 1981

The UK government enlisted scientists and engineers to create its 'Domestic Nuclear Shelters' programme in the early 1980s. This resulted in the production of two guides, which were closely linked to the wider 'Protect and Survive' campaign. The illustrations here are from a slim booklet of easy

Improvised garden shelter using household materials

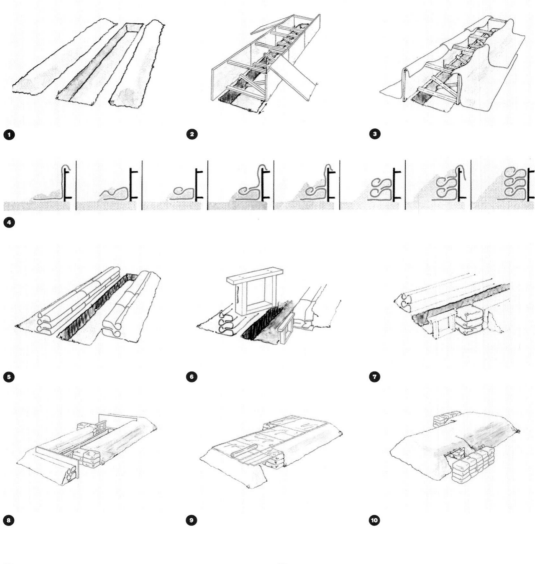

1 Excavate trench
2 Construct temporary walls
3 Position sheeting material
4 Construct earth rolls
5 Remove temporary walls

6 Construct entry/exit frames
7 Sandbags hold material in folded position
8 Construct end earth rolls
9 Position doors and waterproof cover
10 Finish structure with earth cover

to construct, do-it-yourself shelters, which was provided for enthusiastic homeowners. A more comprehensive manual, aimed at professional builders and engineers, was also published, containing blueprints and step-by-step guides for a variety of complex shelters.

The guides were launched early in 1981. In an unusual publicity exercise, the press was invited to view five types of shelter, constructed to the specifications laid out in the manuals, at the Home Defence College in Easingwold, North Yorkshire.

Improvised outdoor shelter using do-it-yourself materials

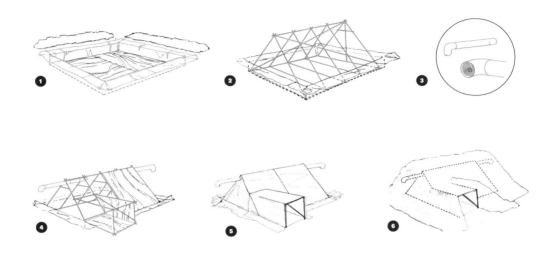

❶ Prepare a trench 2.4 by 2.4 m (8 × 8 ft) and at least 0.5 m (1½ ft) deep. Line it with heavy duty polythene sheeting. Lay a floor of two sheets of plywood ❷ Construct a frame of scaffold poles. This should be as strong as you can make it ❸ You will need to make some provision for ventilation ❹ Add the frame for the entrance tunnel and also the ventilation pipe ❺ Wrap the shelter with overlapping sheets of heavy duty polythene. Make sure the trench lining is within this cover ❻ Finally, cover the shelter with a thick layer of earth. The earth removed from the trench may not be enough for this

Indoor shelter from a manufactured kit

Suitable for homes that have basements or rooms that can be converted into fallout rooms

Outdoor shelter from a manufactured kit

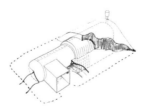

Suitable where there is a garden or other convenient piece of land near the living accommodation

Permanent purpose-built shelter

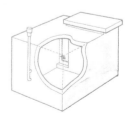

Must be erected by a building contractor under the guidance of a chartered civil/structural engineer

Blast and Fallout

Most of us think we can picture what a nuclear explosion involves: a bright flash of light, a tremendously loud explosion and a mushroom cloud towering over scenes of widespread destruction. The reality is far worse. The flash – brighter than the sun – temporarily blinds anyone looking in its direction. The harmful infrared and ultraviolet radiation that travels with it causes severe burns and eye injuries, and ignites flammable materials such as clothing and curtains. Next comes the blast wave – a high-pressure shock wave radiating out from the explosion, generating high wind speeds and destroying buildings in its path. When the fireball at the centre of the explosion comes into contact with the ground, it drags particles into the air, transforming them into radioactive fallout. Arguably the deadliest effect of the weapon, this fallout then returns to the ground over time, blowing downwind, mixing with rain clouds and being dispersed over a potentially huge area.

Those who picture survivors enduring a return to medieval conditions are only partly correct: in medieval times, people were not blinded and burnt, anxious to the point of psychological incapacity, and eating food and drinking water that would lead to a slow and painful death.

In the event of a nuclear explosion, people would have seconds to find somewhere to hide from the effects of the initial heat and blast. The UK's infamous *Protect and Survive* booklet, prepared in the 1970s, states: 'Use any kind of cover, or lie flat in a ditch and cover the exposed skin of the head and hands.' The US pamphlet *Ten for Survival* simply advises: 'The main idea – Get behind something.' If you survived the blast, there would then be a short period before the fallout arrived. *Protect and Survive* suggests using this time to put out any fires, turn off the gas supply and make your way into your do-it-yourself fallout shelter for at least 48 hours. Beyond that, the public were told to listen to the radio for further instructions – if there was anyone still broadcasting.

Ordinary householders were not the only ones targeted with government advice: agriculture would have a vital role to play in feeding the survivors in a post-apocalyptic world. Booklets such as Ireland's *Bás/Beatha* (*Death/ Life*, 1965) and the UK's *Home Defence and the Farmer* (1958) provide detailed instructions on protecting livestock, crops and farm buildings from deadly fallout.

In the Eastern bloc, colourful posters and civil defence manuals explained the protective values of

① 22 (Joe-17) Soviet underwater nuclear torpedo test, Northern Test Site Novaya Zemlya (NTSNZ), 21 September 1955. ②③④ A model house hit by the shockwave from the 'Annie' nuclear weapons test conducted as part of Operation Upshot-Knothole in Nevada, 17 March 1953. Model towns, known as Survival City or Doom Town, were constructed at the site for the purpose of testing the effects of the blasts.

① ② ③ ④

different types of building materials for communal shelters, how best to hide from a nuclear blast and how to help people decontaminate themselves in a river, should they get a coating of radioactive fallout. They even demonstrated first aid techniques and how to don a gas mask before entering a public shelter. Chinese posters from the 1970s depicted ordinary people working together to construct communal shelters, fleeing into them, en masse, during a surprise nuclear attack and hosing down contaminated buildings afterwards.

The dissolution of the Soviet Union in 1991 brought the Cold War to an end, and with it, the threat of nuclear attack seemed to dissipate. But nuclear weapons still stand ready around the world, aimed at key targets and in sufficient numbers – there are more than 9,000 in active military service – to destroy the world many times over. However safe we might feel, it is chilling to think that we remain a push of a button away from annihilation. We must all hope that the information in the following pages continues to be a curiosity and not a necessity.

Civil Defence Manual of Basic Training: Basic Chemical Warfare, Home Office, UK, 1949

In addition to nuclear war, governments in the early years of the Cold War were concerned with the dangers of chemical and biological attack. This led to the ongoing development of gas masks and NBC (nuclear, biological and chemical) protective clothing. These photographs show the variety of designs available to civil defence forces in the United Kingdom.

1 Helmet respirator, showing the wearer operating the bellows **2** Civilian respirator, showing the arrangement of tape to support the weight of the container and to prevent the face piece from slipping forward **3** Light anti-gas outfit. Note the webbing belt is not standard equipment but is useful in preventing 'ballooning' of the coat in windy weather **4** Taking off the civilian duty respirator **5** Civilian respirator in its carton **6** Showing the correct way of packing the respirator in its carton **7** Preparing to put on the civilian respirator **8** Thrusting the chin into the civilian respirator **9** Taking off the civilian respirator **10** Two women wearing civilian respirators

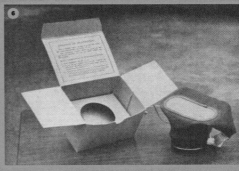

Civilian respirator being worn

'This consists of a mask of thin sheet rubber with a large window of non-inflammable transparent material. The container fits into the face piece and is secured by means of a stout rubber band. The rubber of the mask, being thin and flexible, makes a gas-tight contact with the skin of the face all round. The mask with container attached is held in place by three webbing bands, which pass through a T-shaped buckle at the back of the head.'
Civil Defence Manual of Basic Training: Basic Chemical Warfare, 1949

1 Side straps secured in line with the axis of the container **2** T-buckle not too far down at the back of the head **3** Eye panel well clear of nose **4** Eyes in the middle of the eye panel **5** Snug fit under the chin

Service respirator being worn

'In order to give adequate protection to those in the civil defence services, whose duties may compel them to do strenuous work in high concentration of gas for long periods, the service respirator is fitted with a larger and heavier container than those fitted to respirators already described. It cannot, therefore, be directly fitted to the face piece, but is carried in a haversack on the chest and connected to the face piece by a flexible corrugated rubber tube. Apart from the very high degree of protection it provides, the service respirator gives the wearer the greatest possible freedom of movement and comfort.'
Civil Defence Manual of Basic Training: Basic Chemical Warfare, 1949

❶ Eyes in the centre of the eye panel ❷ Connecting tube slack, allowing free movement of the head without disturbing the fit of the face piece ❸ Chin strap of helmet on the 'point' of the chin ❹ Flap of the haversack open to allow free access to the air container ❺ Haversack well up on the chest

Education for National Survival, Department of Health, Education and Welfare, USA, 1956

The US government created a special manual for education authorities, which aimed to prepare classrooms for nuclear attack. In addition to explaining the effects of the bomb, and where to take shelter, it details the equipment used to detect radiation.

1

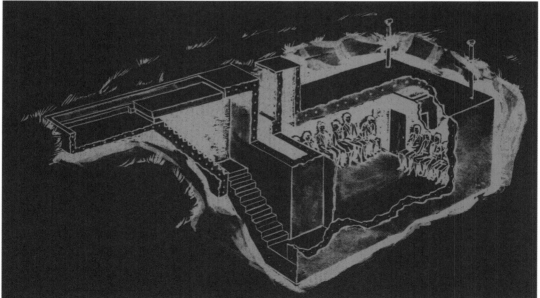

2

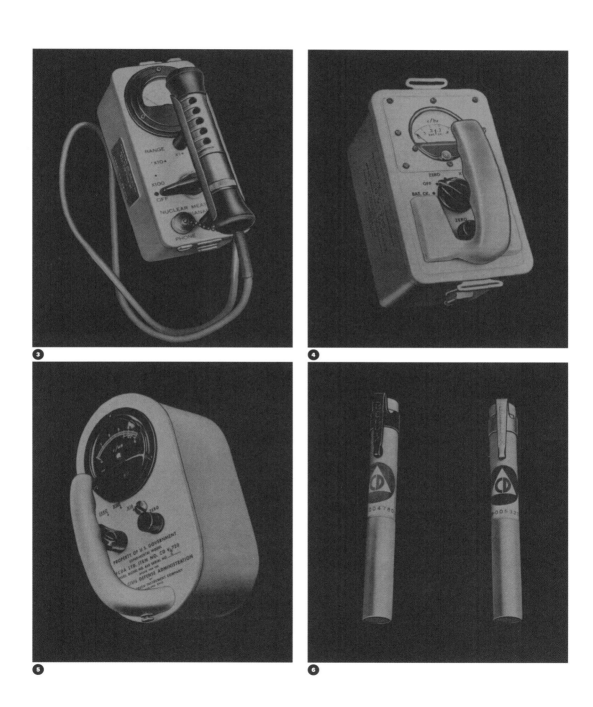

The Hydrogen Bomb,
Home Office, UK, 1957

This booklet was an early response to public interest in the new hydrogen bomb, or H-bomb, which was markedly more destructive than earlier atomic weapons. It sought to clearly set out the facts about how the bomb worked and how to protect yourself.

The danger from HEAT

1 A ground burst **2** Anything that keeps off the sun's heat will help to give protection against the heat of a nuclear bomb. At Hiroshima, for instance, a painted surface was scorched except where it was in the shadow of a wheel **3** Window panes should be white-washed and anything inflammable removed from doorways and windows **4** Otherwise the heat flash will have its best chance to start a fire

The danger from BLAST

1 The blast does not strike like a sudden blow; its action is drawn out, more like a hurricane **2** The stairs would give some protection against falling debris **3** A slit trench with an earth covering protects against blast and radiation

FALL OUT · BURST · SHOCK POWER REDUCED THROUGH EARTH

PATH OF FALL-OUT · MAIN FIRE ZONE (3½–10 MILES) · TOTAL DESTRUCTION · IRREPARABLE DAMAGE · SEVERE TO MODERATE DAMAGE · LIGHT DAMAGE 20–25 MILES · 3½ MILES · 5 MILES · 13 MILES

The danger from

RADIOACTIVITY

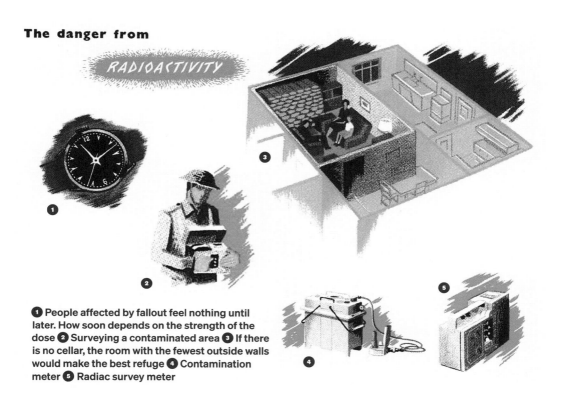

❶ People affected by fallout feel nothing until later. How soon depends on the strength of the dose ❷ Surveying a contaminated area ❸ If there is no cellar, the room with the fewest outside walls would make the best refuge ❹ Contamination meter ❺ Radiac survey meter

❶ In trying to picture what would happen in a nuclear war, many of us attempt to pick out the likely targets. In the process, most of us put our own town high on the list ❷ After a hydrogen bomb explosion, vast numbers of people would be in dire need of help. The Civil Defence Corps is specially organized for this purpose

Estimated Damage Posters, Before and After (1 + 1a), Home Office, UK, 1958

The UK Home Office created these posters in the late 1950s, depicting the same street before and after nuclear attack. They would have been used to show volunteers what to expect.

1 Typical view in centre of city
2 Damage at about 4.8–6.4 km (3–4 mi) from ground burst 10 megaton bomb (=500n)

1

2

Estimated Damage Posters, Before and After (4 + 4a), Home Office, UK, 1958

Stickers were applied to later editions of the 'before and after' posters in order to update the bomb power figures. This reflected the ever-increasing ferocity of nuclear weapons.

1 Typical two-storey domestic property
2 Damage at about 11–16 km (7–10 mi) from ground burst 10 megaton bomb (=500n)

Buildings:
load bearing wall construction

Typical two storey domestic property   4

1

Nominal bomb air burst

6,000 ft. - 8,000 ft.

Buildings: damage to roofs,
windows, partitions etc.

Streets: scattered with light debris

Direction of blast

4a

Damage at about 7-10 miles from ground-burst 10 m.t. bomb (=500 n)

2

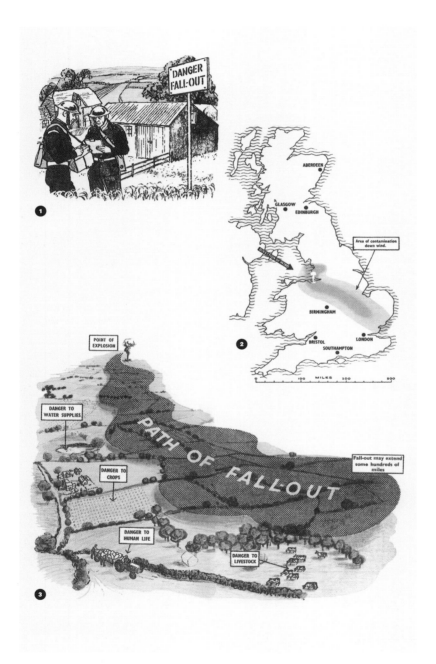

Home Defence and the Farmer, Ministry of Agriculture, Fisheries and Food, UK, 1958

Since agriculture would play a crucial role after a nuclear attack, special attention was paid to equipping farmers with information about the threat. Part of an early 'multimedia' campaign, this 1950s manual formed the basis of an in-depth public information film.

❶ This handbook has been prepared... to present in non-technical language information about radioactive material, called 'fallout', the best assessment that can be made at present of its effect on farming, and to advise on how it might be dealt with **❷** Typical fallout pattern. This diagram illustrates the fallout pattern from an H-bomb supposedly dropped on the north-west coast, with the wind blowing from a generally westerly direction **❸** If this country were to be attacked with nuclear weapons, many farms would be damaged or set on fire, even though they might be well away from where the explosions occurred. In addition, there would be grave risk that highly dangerous radioactive dust (or fallout) resulting from the explosions would be spread over wide areas of the countryside

DANGER FALL-OUT

ABERDEEN

GLASGOW
EDINBURGH

Area of contamination down wind.

DIRECTION OF WIND

BIRMINGHAM

BRISTOL
SOUTHAMPTON
LONDON

MILES 100 200 300

POINT OF EXPLOSION

DANGER TO WATER SUPPLIES

PATH OF FALLOUT

DANGER TO CROPS

Fall-out may extend some hundreds of miles

DANGER TO HUMAN LIFE

DANGER TO LIVESTOCK

Fallout on the Farm, Department of Agriculture, Canada, 1961

Guides provided to farmers focused on how they could ensure that their crops and livestock avoided contamination from radioactive fallout. This manual sets out the steps agricultural workers would have to take to secure safe food supplies for Canada's post-apocalyptic community.

1 You may need a shelter in the barn

2 Have tarpaulins and sacks ready to cover your machinery

3 You could pile earth against buildings, if you have a bulldozer

4 Protect crops harvested before fallout

5 Plough the top soil under to bury fallout

6 Threshing helps to decontaminate cereal crops

7 Sheltered animals have a better chance of survival

8 Livestock may get ill from radiation in their food and water

9 Move livestock indoors as soon as possible

10 Cover open silos or stacks of fodder

11 Store as much water as possible

12 Have fencing ready to confine cattle to a small grazing area

13 Water from a covered well should be safe

14 Try to clip or hose down animals that have fallout on their coats

15 You may have to bury animals that die of radiation sickness

16 Nuclear attack may come in the winter

11 Steps to Survival, Emergency Measures Organization, Canada, 1961

This booklet is part of the *Blueprint for Survival* series. Stark images show the effects of an atomic strike on buildings at various distances and illustrate straightforward advice on protecting yourself from the effects of nuclear weapons.

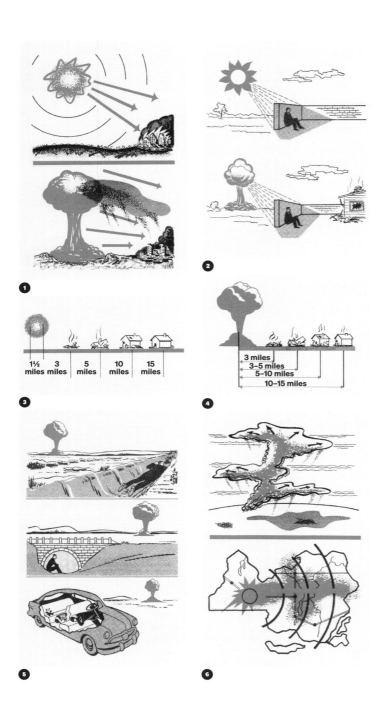

❶ The effects depend on whether the weapon explodes high in the air or on or near the ground. An air burst usually produces more fire, blast and damage, while a ground burst results in a bigger crater and more radioactive fallout ❷ A substantial shield between you and the light will give protection against burns from the heat flash ❸ Serious fires would probably extend up to 14 km (9 mi) and some fires up to 32 km (20 mi) from the point of burst of the bomb ❹ The blast wave travels more slowly than the heat flash. Several seconds may pass after you have seen the light or felt the heat before the blast wave reaches you, depending on the distance you are from the explosion ❺ The pictures show some of the most likely situations in which you may find yourself at the time of a nuclear attack and what you should do. Take shelter in natural terrain, in a culvert or in a car ❻ When a nuclear weapon is exploded on or near the ground, the danger from radioactive particles is greatest... Millions of tons of pulverized earth, stones, buildings and their materials are drawn up into the fireball and become radioactive. Some of the heavier particles spill out around the point of explosion. The rest are sucked up into the mushroom cloud, which rises as high as 30,480 m (100,000 ft). This radioactive material is then carried by the wind until it settles to earth. This we call fallout

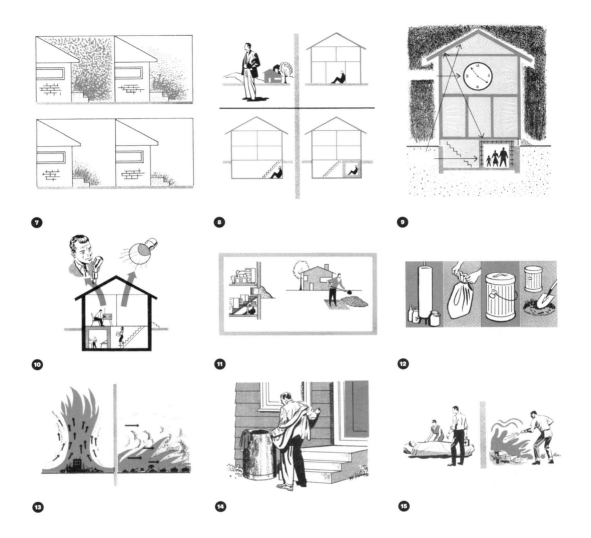

⑦ The radioactivity in fallout weakens rapidly in the first hours after an explosion. This weakening is called decay ⑧ Therefore, if you stay in a shelter in the initial days after an explosion, you avoid the strongest radiation ⑨ The most effective protection is to place some heavy material between yourself and the fallout ⑩ A battery-powered radio is essential because electricity may be cut off. An emergency broadcasting plan has been prepared ⑪ One of the simplest ways of improvizing an anti-blast shelter is to build a lean-to against a work bench or heavy table... or if you have sufficient warning of attack, dig yourself a trench in the yard, although not too close to any buildings that might collapse into it ⑫ Use the hot water tank as a source of water, put human waste in plastic bags, use a garbage can for waste, bury waste and garbage when safe ⑬ Fire storms take place only under special conditions. The possibility of fire storms in Canadian cities is so slight that the fire authorities discount them. The possibility of conflagration is much greater. Fire storm: like a furnace, everything is consumed. Conflagration: like a forest fire, it burns everything in its path ⑭ If you suspect you have been exposed to fallout, you will not be a danger to others if you carefully get rid of your outer clothes and wash ⑮ If an attack takes place and you survive the immediate effects... you will then be in danger from fire and fallout. But you should have about 30 minutes before fallout starts to come down to put out any small fires that have started and give first aid to those that need it

Survival in Likely Target Areas, Emergency Measures Organization, Canada, 1962

Another booklet in the *Blueprint for Survival* series, this guide focuses on survival advice for those in the cross-hairs of Soviet missiles. Dramatic illustrations show how objects found in an urban setting could offer protection from the effects of a nuclear burst.

SURVIVAL IN LIKELY TARGET AREAS

BLUEPRINT FOR SURVIVAL No. 5

①

Effects of 5 megaton blast on exposed people

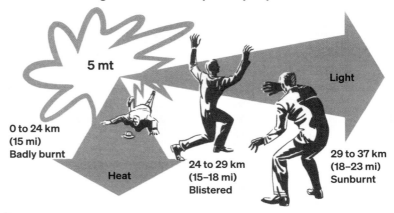

5 mt

Light

0 to 24 km (15 mi)
Badly burnt

Heat

24 to 29 km (15–18 mi)
Blistered

29 to 37 km (18–23 mi)
Sunburnt

①

Effects of 5 megaton blast on buildings

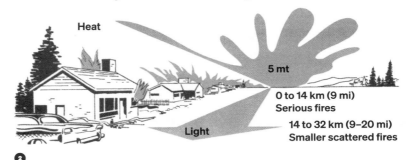

Heat

5 mt

0 to 14 km (9 mi)
Serious fires

14 to 32 km (9–20 mi)
Smaller scattered fires

Light

②

Immediate radiation from a 5 megaton blast

① The dangers of an H-bomb explosion: light and heat, immediate radiation, blast (known collectively as immediate effects) and radioactive fallout
② Blast: immediately after the light, heat and radiation, a powerful blast wave moves out in all directions from the centre of the explosion
③ Immediate radiation: most people within 3.2 km (2 mi) of the explosion who survive the blast and fire will die from immediate radiation unless they have adequate protection against it

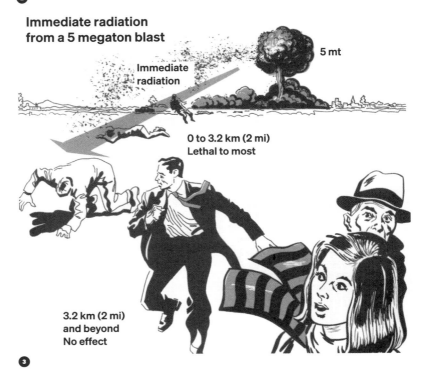

Immediate radiation

5 mt

0 to 3.2 km (2 mi)
Lethal to most

3.2 km (2 mi) and beyond
No effect

③

Effects of the blast on buildings

0 to 4.8 km (3 mi)
Complete destruction

4.8 to 8 km (3–5 mi)
Beyond repair

8 to 16 km (5–10 mi)
Major repairs required

16 to 24 km (10–15 mi)
Light damage

④

Chances of survival in a basement

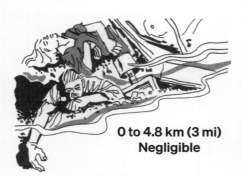

0 to 4.8 km (3 mi)
Negligible

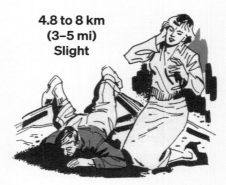

4.8 to 8 km
(3–5 mi)
Slight

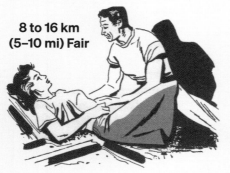

8 to 16 km
(5–10 mi) Fair

16 to 24 km
(10–15 mi)
Good

⑤

4 Buildings and the blast: unlike the blast pressure from conventional explosions, which lasts for a fraction of a second, the blast pressure from an H-bomb lasts for several seconds. This sustained pressure crushes buildings or bursts into them and causes them to explode **5** Sheltering from the blast: those without anti-blast shelters could increase their chances of survival by improvising protection against flying materials and collapsing buildings **6** Outdoor sheltering advice: your first indication of attack could be a dazzling, almost overpowering light. In the open, all you can do is fall flat or dive into a ditch, gutter or behind natural protection **7** Home sheltering advice: cover your head with your arms, keep your eyes shut and stay low. Remember the destructive blast wave will follow shortly **8** Building sheltering advice: inside a building, one of the greatest dangers will be from flying glass. Get behind furniture, in a corner or on the floor out of the line of the window **9** Transport sheltering advice: open your car window and have all passengers lie on the floors or seats covered with blankets or coats. At the first flash of brilliant light – duck

Attack without warning: Survival positions

6

7

8

9

Radioactive fallout travels with the wind; it does not respect national borders. Despite being officially neutral, the Irish government recognized that any nuclear exchange involving the UK would most likely impact their people, too. Ireland created

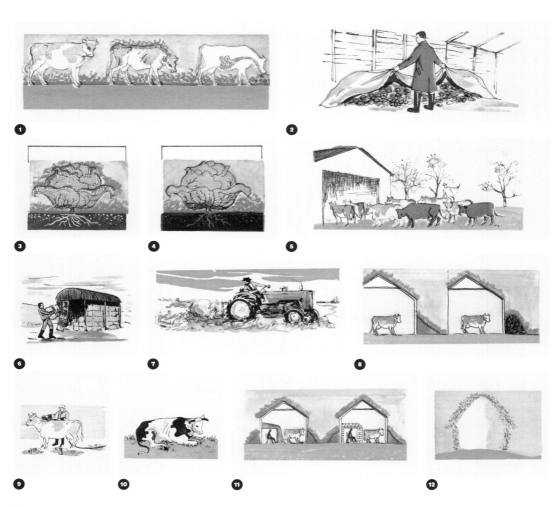

1 Radiation from surrounding (left) radioactive dust on the body (centre) and radioactive dust inside the body (right) **2** Plastic sheeting and tarpaulins are very suitable as coverings **3** Plants can be contaminated on their surfaces **4** Worse still, growing plants can absorb radioactive material from the soil **5** Advance warning: bring in livestock and poultry **6** Animals should be brought in under cover for at least the first two days of fallout... If you are short of room, you might consider using an adapted hay shed **7** Cut and remove contaminated grass **8** Where possible, bank up clay, stones, turf or any other convenient materials against the wall **9** Animals that were exposed during fallout will have the fallout dust trapped in their coats. Hose them down or clip their hair to get rid of the dust **10** Animals that were out in the fallout will have suffered hidden damage from the radioactive rays... they may fall ill and die in a few weeks **11** Cows will be in great pain during the refuge period unless you make arrangements to milk them **12** Haystacks or stacked grain that were left uncovered in the open would be contaminated – but only the top few inches

a civil defence force, which provided advice on nuclear attack during the Cold War, and it has remained operational into the 21st century. In the 1960s, it published *Bás/Beatha* (*Death/Life*), which set out the risks of nuclear attack and defence against its effects. This guide is unusual in that it combines householder and agricultural advice in the same booklet. This makes sense considering more than half of Ireland's population lived in rural communities at the start of the 1960s.

13 For hatching, try and breed from birds that were indoors during fallout **14** When you are doing a job that stirs up dust (threshing, stacking hay, etc.) take extra precautions: gloves, cuffs tied, cloth around nose and mouth, sound boots **15** Apples – peel and wash **16** Potatoes – peel and wash **17** Peas – remove pods **18** Lettuce and cabbage – remove leaves, use heart **19** Leafed vegetables – do not use **20** Soft fruits – do not use **21** Preserve eggs with waterglass [sodium silicate] **22** Make butter and keep it to be tested for contamination. Feed the skim milk to pigs or bullocks (it will not affect their flesh) **23** Wash radioactive dust off roofs, paths and hard surfaces

Surviving Doomsday, Colin Bruce Sibley, UK, 1977

Unimpressed by public information campaigns around nuclear attack, C. Bruce Sibley created his own manual. *Surviving Doomsday* explains how ordinary people can construct a homemade suit to protect themselves from nuclear fallout.

Homemade protective suit

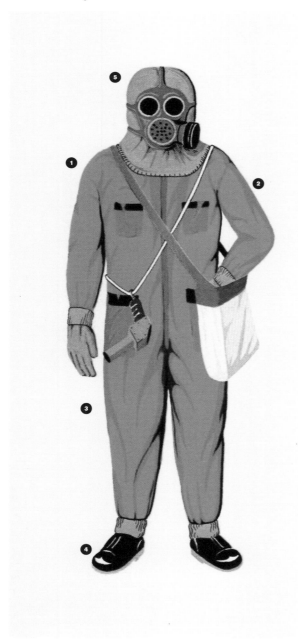

1 Obtain or make a one-piece suit (boiler suit, tracksuit, ski suit or overall). Preferably zip fastened. Also obtain a pair of thick cotton socks and gloves. Make a good balaclava helmet to cover the head, neck and most of the face **2** Heat 9 l (2 gal) of water to 60°C (140°F) then add 2.2 l (½ gal) of liquid washing up detergent, 0.3 l (½ pt) of disinfectant and 0.45 kg (1 lb) of household soap peelings. Mix well. Immerse the suit and other items and leave to soak for 15 minutes. DO NOT BOIL. Remove impregnated clothing and dry. DO NOT BRUSH OR IRON **3** IMPORTANT: A duplicate set of underclothing must be worn beneath the protective suit to prevent skin irritation **4** Boots should be made of thick rubber. The interior lining should be soaked with liquid detergent and left to dry **5** Civil defence respirators can be obtained from manufacturers of industrial protective equipment. Homemade masks consisting of dampened gauze, foam or cloth covering the nose and mouth are only effective at removing fallout dust, NOT biochemical agents. This type of homemade mask must be renewed at frequent intervals because of contamination. Ingenious survivors may like to consider adapting racing helmets for use as a homemade fallout mask

Backed by science and statistics, the manual goes into the effects of nuclear attack in great detail, and also expounds on shelter construction and developments in 'exotic weaponry'. It further delves into the threat from chemical and biological weapons as well as nuclear attack. Keen to share knowledge around disaster preparedness, Sibley later founded two magazines for individual preppers: *Protect and Survive Monthly* and *Practical Civil Defence*.

Body portals: How agents enter the body

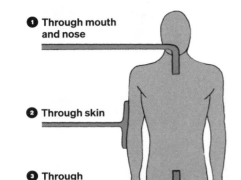

1 Through mouth and nose

2 Through skin

3 Through excretory exits

Sources of possible radiation hazard

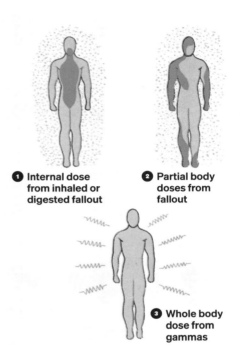

1 Internal dose from inhaled or digested fallout

2 Partial body doses from fallout

3 Whole body dose from gammas

Development of a nuclear explosion

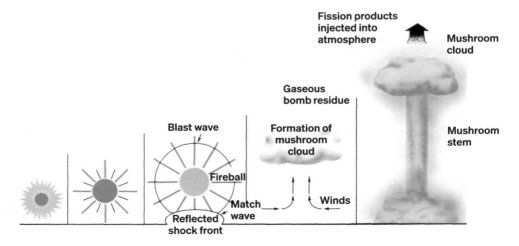

Fission products injected into atmosphere

Mushroom cloud

Gaseous bomb residue

Mushroom stem

Blast wave

Formation of mushroom cloud

Fireball

Match wave

Winds

Reflected shock front

Protect and Survive, Home Office, UK, 1980

Originally intended to be issued as part of a wider public information campaign when nuclear attack seemed inevitable, *Protect and Survive* gained notoriety when it was instead made public in 1980, following newspaper reports and an investigation on a popular BBC documentary programme.

❶ Even the safest room in your home is not safe enough... You will need to block up windows in the room and any other openings, and to make the outside walls thicker, and also to thicken the floor above you ❷ If you live in a block of flats, there are other factors to consider. If the block is more than five storeys high, do not shelter in the top two floors... If your flat is in a block of four storeys or less, the basement or ground floor will give you the best protection ❸ Bungalows and similar single-storey homes will not give much protection... select a place in your home that is furthest from the roof and outside walls ❹ Make a lean-to with sloping doors taken from rooms above or strong boards rested against an inner wall. Prevent them from slipping by fixing a length of wood along the floor. Build further protection of bags and boxes of earth and sand... on the slope of your refuge ❺ Use tables if they are large enough to provide you all with shelter. Surround and cover them with heavy furniture filled with sand, earth, books or clothing ❻ Use the cupboard under the stairs if it is in your fallout room. Put bags of earth or sand on the stairs and along the wall of the cupboard ❼ You will need enough water for the family for 14 days... seal or cover all

The early publication of the manual by Margaret Thatcher's newly formed government was intended to be a show of strength; instead, it led to widespread criticism from the press and public. The manual and its accompanying videos were parodied in popular culture, including in the Frankie Goes to Hollywood hit single 'Two Tribes'. In the United Kingdom, *Protect and Survive* remains among the best-known cultural artefacts of nuclear preparedness, having marked a turning point in public attitudes to civil defence.

you can. Anything that has fallout dust on it will be contaminated and dangerous to eat or drink **8** Stock enough food for 14 days. Choose foods that can be eaten cold, that keep fresh and that are tinned or well wrapped **9** Your radio will be your only link with the outside world. So take a spare one with you if you can **10** Keep these items just outside the fallout room: a dustbin for temporary storage of sealed bags of waste and a second dustbin for food remains, empty tins and other rubbish **11** Keep buckets of water ready on each floor... Coat windows inside with diluted emulsion paint in a light colour so that they will reflect away much of the heat flash, even if the blast that follows will shatter them... Remove boxes, firewood and materials that will burn easily and that are close to the outside of the house **12** After a nuclear attack, there will be a short period before fallout starts to descend. Use this time to do essential tasks... Go round the house and put out any small fires using mains water if you can **13** Do not flush lavatories but store the clean water they contain by taping up the handles or removing the chains **14** Everyone must go to the fallout room and stay inside the inner refuge, keeping the radio tuned for government advice and instructions

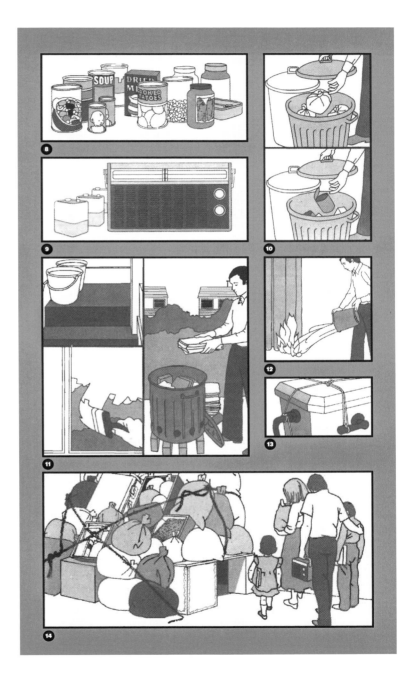

Army: *Survive to Fight*, Director of Army Training, UK, 1983

Official survival manuals were not the preserve of the general public. Military personnel were issued with their own guides to surviving nuclear attack. The *Survive to Fight* series instructed soldiers on personal protection from NBC (nuclear, biological and chemical) attack.

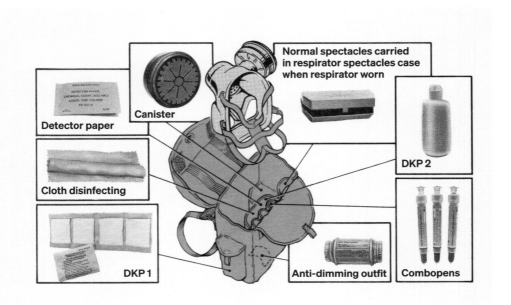

Normal spectacles carried in respirator spectacles case when respirator worn

Detector paper

Canister

Cloth disinfecting

DKP 1

DKP 2

Anti-dimming outfit

Combopens

①

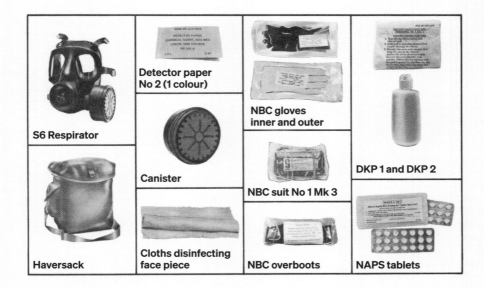

S6 Respirator

Haversack

Detector paper No 2 (1 colour)

Canister

Cloths disinfecting face piece

NBC gloves inner and outer

NBC suit No 1 Mk 3

NBC overboots

DKP 1 and DKP 2

NAPS tablets

②

3. Nuclear War

① This illustration shows where the items of individual protection equipment that are not worn should be stored in a haversack.
② Items of individual protection equipment. Soldiers were advised to 'study the pictures so that you can recognize them without difficulty'.

① First aid for nerve agent poisoning
② First aid for choking agent poisoning
③ First aid for blood agent poisoning
④ First aid for blister agent casualties

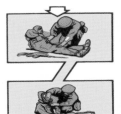

- Inject with combopen every 15 minutes until casualty's devices are used or he recovers
- Put the used devices back in the haversack so others will know how many have been employed

- If he is conscious:
- Give him the diazepam tablet from the combopen
- Don't give him NAPS tablets

- If he stops breathing, decontaminate his face and give artificial respiration:
- With the portable resuscitator when there is a vapour hazard
- Manually when no resuscitator is available
- Mouth to mouth when there is no vapour hazard

- Evacuate him for further medical aid

①

- Make sure you and the casualty have the appropriate degree of NBC protection

- Keep him warm

- If the vapour hazard remains and you have a casualty bag, put the casualty in it and remove his respirator

- Evacuate him for further medical aid

②

- Make sure you and the casualty have the appropriate degree of NBC protection

- If he stops breathing, give artificial respiration:
- With the portable resuscitator when there is a vapour hazard
- Manually when no resuscitator is available
- Mouth to mouth when there is no vapour hazard

- Keep him warm

- Evacuate him for further medical aid

③

- Make sure you and the casualty have the appropriate degree of NBC protection (blister agent is always persistent and may remain a contact hazard for at least 36 hours)

- If the casualty has agent in his eyes, flush them with plenty of water. You must only do this when you are certain you started your first aid within 5 minutes of him being contaminated
- Replace respirator

- Check the casualty for reddened skin around the hairline, behind the ears and on his hands
- Decontaminate suspected areas with DKP 1 and try and swab off the Fuller's earth powder with water

- Dress blisters with your shell dressing after you have decontaminated the skin; cover with chemical-proof material
- On no account should you break the blisters

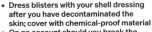

- Evacuate him for further medical aid

④

Civil Defence (Гражданская оборона), Soviet Union, 1986

This Soviet civil defence manual is more comprehensive than most of its Western counterparts. On one hand, it offers practical advice on decontamination after nuclear attack: removing deadly radioactive fallout from clothes,

Decontamination of food and water

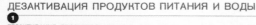

ДЕЗАКТИВАЦИЯ ПРОДУКТОВ ПИТАНИЯ И ВОДЫ   46

❶ ДЕЗАКТИВАЦИЯ ПРОДУКТОВ ПИТАНИЯ—ЭТО УДАЛЕНИЕ РАДИОАКТИВНЫХ ВЕЩЕСТВ ПУТЕМ СНЯТИЯ ПОВЕРХНОСТНОГО СЛОЯ ПРОДУКТОВ, ОБМЫВАНИЯ ИХ ВОДОЙ

ВСЕ РАБОТЫ ПО ДЕЗАКТИВАЦИИ ВЫПОЛНЯЮТСЯ С ИСПОЛЬЗОВАНИЕМ СРЕДСТВ ИНДИВИДУАЛЬНОЙ ЗАЩИТЫ: ПРОТИВОГАЗА ИЛИ ВАТНО-МАРЛЕВОЙ ПОВЯЗКИ, ПЕРЧАТОК И Т. П.

СПОСОБЫ ДЕЗАКТИВАЦИИ ПРОДУКТОВ ПИТАНИЯ И ВОДЫ

❷ Промывание консервных банок горячей водой с мылом

❸ Протирание мокрой тряпкой и обильное обмывание проточной водой плотно закрытых термосов или бидонов с продовольствием

❹ Очистка пылесосами или перекладывание в чистую тару продовольствия в мешкотаре

❺ Крупу высыпать из пакета в дуршлаг и тщательно промыть

❻ Срезание поверхностного загрязненного слоя с твердых жиров; обмывание водой мяса

ВОДУ ДЕЗАКТИВИРУЮТ ТРЕМЯ СПОСОБАМИ:

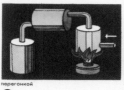

❼ перегонкой

❽ отстаиванием

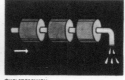

❾ фильтрованием

Загрязненные радиоактивными веществами выше допустимых норм молоко и молочные продукты перерабатывают на масло, сгущенное молоко или творог

❶ Food is decontaminated by removing radioactive substances from its surface or washing it in water. All decontamination work is done while wearing personal protective gear: a gas mask or a cotton and gauze face covering, gloves, etc. ❷ Canned goods: wash with hot water and soap ❸ Thermoses and food containers: tightly close, then use a damp cloth to wipe them down and wash thoroughly in running water ❹ Bagged goods: vacuum off the bag or transfer contents to a new, clean bag ❺ Grains: empty them into a strainer and rinse thoroughly ❻ Solid fats: cut off the contaminated surface layer. Meat: wash with water. Milk and dairy products that have been contaminated above permissible standards should be processed into butter, condensed milk and quark. Three methods for decontaminating water are: ❼ Distilling ❽ Settling ❾ Filtering

skin, foodstuffs and buildings. On the other, it demonstrates the thorough and coordinated planning that the Soviet state put into preparation for nuclear war. With specialized vehicles, equipment and clothing, the manual depicts Soviet authorities as being thoroughly prepared to deal with the effects of nuclear weapons. This suggests that the Soviet Union saw civil defence not only as a way of helping people survive nuclear attack, but also as a means of ensuring the continued survival of the state.

Decontamination of clothing and shoes

ДЕЗАКТИВАЦИЯ ОДЕЖДЫ И ОБУВИ ПРОИЗВОДИТСЯ:

на площадках дезактивации одежды и обуви пункта специальной обработки
1. Одежда, не поддающаяся дезактивации 2. Контроль полноты дезактивации 3. Склад имущества, не поддающегося дезактивации 4. Дезактивация защитной одежды 5. Дезактивация одежды 6. Ёмкости для воды 7. Дезактивация противогазов 8. Дезактивация обуви (А – чистая, Б – грязная половины площадки)

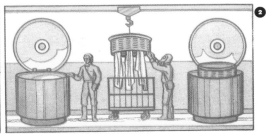

на станциях обеззараживания одежды на базе механических прачечных

Дезактивация одежды и обуви производится выколачиванием, обметанием, вытряхиванием или протиранием дезактивирующими растворами, а при их отсутствии – водой. После обработки производится дозиметрический контроль. При обнаружении зараженности выше допустимой нормы дезактивацию следует повторить

Для обеззараживания применяются вода и 0,15—0,30%-е водные растворы моющих средств

❶ The decontamination of clothing and shoes is performed at special treatment sites ❷ Clothing disinfection stations are located at industrial laundry facilities ❸ Clothing and shoes are decontaminated by beating, brushing, shaking or wiping with a decontamination solution or, in its absence, with water. After treatment, a dosimetry check is performed. If contamination is detected to be above normal, decontamination must be repeated ❹ For disinfection, use water and a 0.15–0.30 per cent detergent solution

4. Alien Invasion

Alien Invasion

We Come in Peace 220
Is There Anyone Out There? 234
What Is the Truth? 240

①

4. Alien Invasion

Now You See It, Now You Don't*
Preparing for Alien Invasion

* 'Now You See It, Now You Don't' is the title of a classified memo written by US Captain Henry S. Shields about an US air crew's 'interesting, and possibly disturbing' UFO encounter in 1976.

① A strange object hovers over Hillsdale, Michigan, 1966. The military claimed it was swamp gas, an explanation witnesses refused to accept.

The arrival of aliens would be an astonishing upheaval that would fundamentally change global society forever. Yet visitors from space are traditionally the subject of Hollywood movies rather than official emergency plans. Naturally, governments do not admit to preparing for contact with extraterrestrial beings, let alone a full-scale invasion. Alien encounters are strictly the domain of screenwriters, sci-fi novelists, fantasists and the bemused – or so official channels would have us believe. But, for all the bureaucratic denials, it is a fact that the world's governments have asked questions about flying saucers, funded attempts at communication with aliens and spent significant time and public money analysing the threat unidentified flying objects (UFOs) pose to national security. From hotlines staffed by intelligence officials to messages beamed into the cosmos, governments around planet Earth have taken the possibility of an alien invasion seriously. With the resulting reports classified at the highest levels of secrecy, many public investigations into threats from beyond the stars are instead carried out by plucky amateurs – with various degrees of scientific rigour and credulity.

We Come in Peace

Who or what are aliens? Arguably, they are simply the latest in a long line of strange creatures that exist at the very fringes of human thought. Only a relatively small number of people claim to have had their own close encounters; for most of us, aliens are a purely cultural phenomenon, experienced through the stories we tell one another. In that sense, they have inherited the mantle from a litany of otherworldly beings stretching back through folklore, including fairies, elves, djinn, angels and demons. Like these antecedents, aliens are often depicted as humanoid, but with powers beyond those of ordinary people, and with ambiguous, mischievous or even malign motives.

Today, the alien from outer space is synonymous with the 'grey': a particular species of being, named for its pallid grey skin. Frequently portrayed as bald, shorter and thinner than a human adult, and with a tiny slit for a mouth, the unsettling, expressionless grey is a familiar trope in Western culture. However, this was not always the case. For most of the 20th century, aliens took a variety of forms and their appearance was by no means as culturally fixed as it is today. Greys were, for a long time, one type among many: in the 1950s, they made up only three per cent of reported otherworldly encounters. Since the 1950s, witnesses have described more than 50 types of creature, including 'walking tombstones', gelatinous blobs, blonde-haired 'Nordics', humanoid lizards and unfeasibly large insectoids.

The 20th century saw frequent waves of UFO sightings, often reflecting the human technology of the day. As people began to spend more time in the air, and flying machines became increasingly complex, we looked to the skies – and saw more than just ourselves. While aliens were busy invading human culture, we started to catch glimpses of their vehicles in the sky.

The sightings began in earnest at the end of the 19th century, with mysterious airships being reported across the United States. While many

1 Betty and Barney Hill claimed to have been abducted by alien beings in 1961.
2 Ralph Ditter, a barber from Zanesville, Ohio, points at the UFO he claims he photographed in 1967.
3 US pilots, including Kenneth Arnold (centre), examine a photograph of an alleged UFO. Reports of Arnold's sighting in 1947 introduced the term 'flying saucer'.
4 Dr J. Allen Hynek, chief scientific advisor in the US government's UFO investigations, holds a blurry photograph of the Moon and Venus.

stories from this period are likely to have been hoaxes, some seem remarkably modern in their details. An unusual airship ran into trouble into Aurora, Texas, in 1897, crashing into a windmill and breaking up into fragments of an unknown metal. The pilot, said to be 'not of this earth', was buried in the town's cemetery. In the early 1970s, *Dallas Times Herald* journalist and UFO investigator Bill Case returned to the town, where he found a grave marker with a saucer shape carved on it. His metal detector picked up strong signals from the plot, but when he returned later to show a friend, the stone was gone and any metal had been carefully removed.

Phantom airship sightings continued into World War I, although official investigations often found the mysterious lights in the sky to have prosaic explanations, such as being misidentified planets. During World War II, Allied pilots reported a variety of unusual sightings under the umbrella term 'foo fighters', sometimes in the belief that they were encountering experimental aircraft flown by the Axis powers. While the Nazis did have prototypes of unusually shaped aircraft, it is highly unlikely that they were flown in combat. Again, official reports attributed the sightings to unusual atmospheric phenomena or to the psychological and physiological effects of aerial combat.

The years following the war were when the modern UFO phenomenon began to come into its own. In June 1947, pilot Kenneth Arnold reported seeing a fleet of nine UFOs flying past Mount Rainier, an active volcano in Washington state. His description of the fantastic objects' shape and motion led to the terms 'flying disc' and 'flying saucer' entering the public imagination. The following month, a military weather balloon crashed at Roswell, New Mexico. After an initial statement from the public relations officer at Roswell Army Air Field that they had captured a flying disc, the *Roswell Daily Record* ran the headline 'RAAF Captures Flying Saucer'. The erroneous official 'confirmation' of a captured disc sparked more interest in the crash and cemented the event's legendary status among believers.

Greys initially made their mark with the first widely reported abduction incident. In 1961, Betty and Barney Hill were driving on US Route 3 when they saw a strange object in the sky, stopped to take a better look and were shocked to observe small creatures working inside. Under hypnosis two years later, they recalled being abducted by aliens, who were described as 'classic' greys, albeit wearing contemporary fashion. Steven Spielberg's movie *Close Encounters of the Third Kind* (1977) seems to have taken cues from the Hills' experience, depicting the aliens in a similar form and number. Ten years later, Whitley Strieber's personal story of alien abduction, *Communion*, prominently featured a classic grey on the cover. Underground artist Bill Barker's 'Schwa' alien head symbol became

⑤ The debut issue of the French UFO magazine *INFO OVNI*, 1975, depicts an alien visitation. ⑥ This issue of *UFO-QUEBEC* magazine from 1976 shows a similar, if slightly more menacing, scene. ⑦ An alien abduction situation features on the cover of *UFO Information*, a Swedish magazine.

⑧ Spanish UFO publication *Stendek* depicts an alien craft landing at Puente de Herrera, Spain. ⑨ *Lumières Dans la Nuit*, founded in 1958, is one of France's longest-running UFO publications.

⑤

⑥

⑦

⑧

⑨

popular in the early 1990s, and greys went on to appear in shows such as *The X-Files* in the mid to late 1990s, cementing them further as the de facto Western depiction of extraterrestrials.

What was it about the 20th century that led aliens to become so culturally conspicuous? Rapid advances in technology meant that old folklore gained a new metallic sheen. As humanity set its sights on space after World War II, we may well have had cause to reconsider our place in the universe – and our relative insignificance. Moreover, as the threat of East-West nuclear conflict increased, aliens became a powerful psychological proxy for 'the other': strange beings like us, but different, who had mastered forces we could not hope to stop, who would arrive in shining aerial craft and whose actions were unpredictable and malevolent. The notion of alien invasion was a safe way to explore a more legitimate fear of conquest by forces closer to home.

If we suspend disbelief for a moment and take it as read that aliens are genuine creatures from beyond the stars, we must consider why they would choose to invade Earth. Those who have claimed to have encountered beings from other worlds can provide some clues. A common theme reported by early abductees was that the visitors, who were not only technologically but also spiritually more advanced than us, wanted to warn humanity about its more destructive impulses: world wars, nuclear weapons and the destruction of the environment. Towards the end of the 20th century, things took a darker turn, with the rise of the alien abduction narrative most closely associated with the greys: they are here to experiment on humans, to create alien-human hybrids, to mutilate cattle and to generally cause trouble. The variety of reported motives could be seen to undermine the validity of the sightings. However, some would argue that these kinds of alien encounter are simply evidence that we have been invaded by several distinct species.

⑩ A formation of four glowing objects passes over Salem, Massachusetts, at night, 1952. **⑪** A supposedly mysterious disc races over a valley in Riverside, California, 1951. **⑫** Passaic, New Jersey, is visited by a purported interstellar craft, 1952. **⑬** One of the controversial photographs of a UFO taken by Paul and Evelyn Trent at their farm in McMinnville, Oregon, 1950.

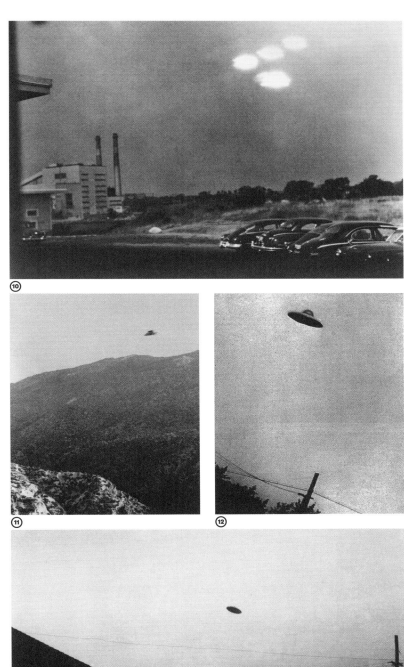

⑩

⑪

⑫

⑬

The UFO Evidence, National Investigations Committee on Aerial Phenomena (NICAP), USA, 1964

The National Investigations Committee on Aerial Phenomena (NICAP) was set up in the 1950s as a nonprofit organization to investigate UFO phenomenon. It collected reports of sightings and encounters for nearly three decades. The

UFO Shape	Bottom View	Bottom Angle	Side View
1. Flat Disc A — October 1954, Cox 2 July 1952, Newhouse B — 9 July 1947, Johnson 14 July 1952, Nash		A B oval	A — lens-shaped B — lens-shaped
2. Domed Disc A — 21 September 1958, Fitzgerald 24 April 1962, Gasslein B — 11 May 1950, Trent 7 August 1952, Jansen		A B hat-shaped	A — World War I helmet B
3. Saturn Disc A — 4 October 1954, Saladin 16 January 1958, Trindade 2 October 1961, Harris B — 20 February 1956, Moore	A B elliptical or winged oval	diamond-shaped	Saturn-shaped
4. Hemispherical Disc 24 September 1958, Redmond 21 January 1961 Pulliam 7 February 1961, Walley		parachute	mushroom or half moon
5. Flattened Sphere 1 October 1948, Gorman 27 April 1950, Adickes 9 October 1951, C.A.A.			sometimes with peak
6. Spherical March 1945, Delarof 20 January 1952, Baller 12 October 1961, Edwards	metallic-appearing ball	ball of glowing light	
7. Elliptical 20 December 1958, Aboraen 2 November 1957, Levelland 13 August 1960, Carson	football or egg-shaped		
8. Triangular 7 May 1956, G.O.C. 22 May 1960, Majorca			teardrop
9. Cylindrical 1 August 1946, Puckett 23 July 1948, Chiles	cigar-shaped	**10. Light Source Only** star-like or planet-like	

①

group believed the US government was hiding the truth and had some success in pushing for Washington to address the issue. *The UFO Evidence* condensed a huge volume of data into one report, which was sent to every member of Congress in an attempt to generate momentum around the issue. The illustrations here, taken from the report, show different types of flying disc reported to NICAP, and different styles of flight paths witnesses claimed to have seen.

UFO flight paths

① The diagrams in this identification table are 'hypothetical constructions, generalized from hundreds of UFO reports', and 'represent with reasonable accuracy virtually all UFOs which have been reliably described in any detail'. The date of the sighting and the name of the reporter (or sometimes the location) associated with each type appear in the lefthand column.

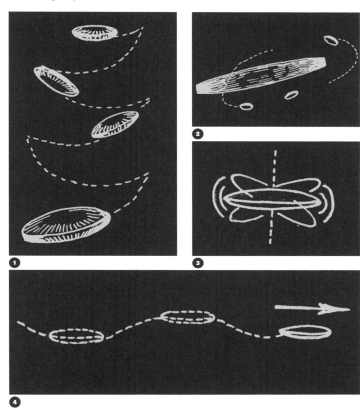

❶ Pendulum motion
❷ Satellite objects
❸ Wobble on axis
❹ Oscillatory flight

UFO flight paths: Witness sightings

❶ 5:15 pm, 8 January 1959. 1.6 km (1 mi) north of Illinois-Wisconsin state line on US Route 14. Movement: slow descent, then shot off at tremendous speed ❷ 5:00 pm, 2 October 1958. Delaware Water Gap, near Blairstown, New Jersey. Movement: rapid gyrations

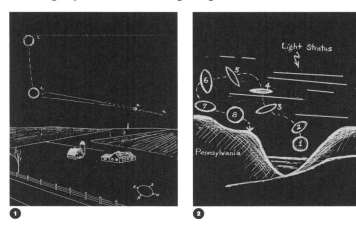

Facts About Unidentified Flying Objects, Library of Congress Legislative Reference Service, USA, 1966

Reporting, investigating and analysing UFO sightings

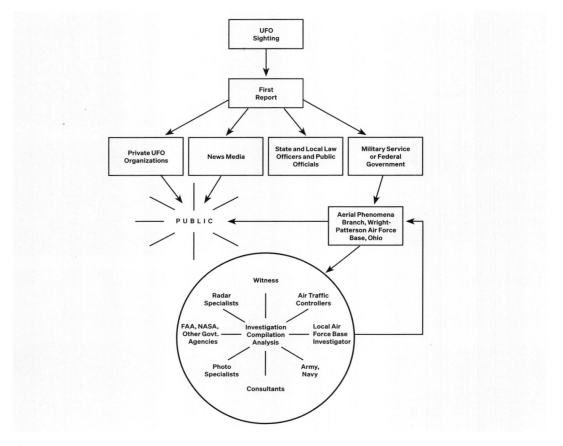

UFO sightings by year, 1815–1915

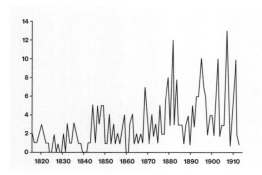

UFO sightings by year, 1947–65

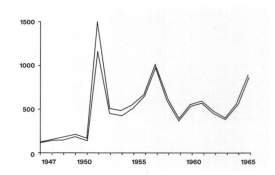

The US Library of Congress published this report to set out the facts about UFOs in 1966. It charts the history of unexplained aerial sightings going back as far as 1815, based on the work of UFO researcher Jacques Vallée. It also analyses the processes by which the public came to know about sightings, and describes the shapes of some of the most commonly spotted objects, putting them into the categories shown here.

Varieties of shape of UFO

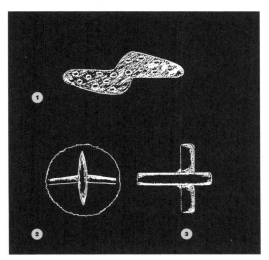

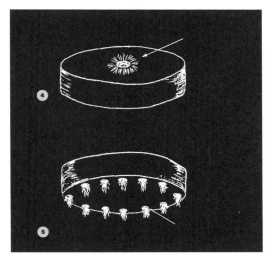

1 Propeller shape **2** Aircraft shape, option 1
3 Aircraft shape, option 2

4 Elliptical or disc shape, view from above, showing flashing light **5** Elliptical or disc shape, view from below, showing portholes

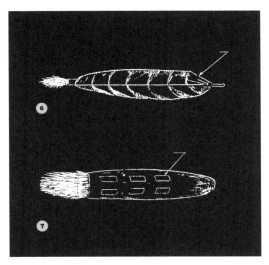

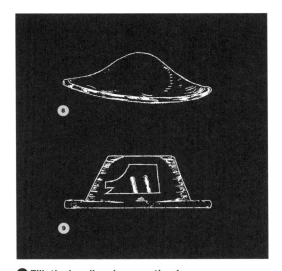

6 Cigar shape, option 1, showing windshield
7 Cigar shape, option 2, showing lighted windows

8 Elliptical or disc shape, option 1
9 Elliptical or disc shape, option 2, side view

Aids to Identification of Flying Objects, Air Force, USA, 1968

It can be surprisingly difficult to correctly interpret what we think we see in the sky, particularly when trying to judge size and distance, or under unusual atmospheric conditions. Through their intensive investigation of flying objects in the 1950s and 1960s, the US authorities found that the vast

Normal atmospheric conditions

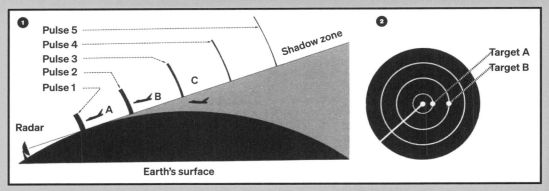

❶ In certain instances, UFOs have been reflected on radarscopes, both ground and airborne... Certain meteorological and astronomical conditions will present radar returns that are unusual. Radar waves must travel through Earth's atmosphere where, like light waves, they may be bent by unusual temperature and moisture conditions. The figure above shows the transmission of a radar pulse under normal atmospheric conditions

❷ The radarscope will show Targets A and B at normal range, but will not pick up Target C

Abnormal atmospheric conditions

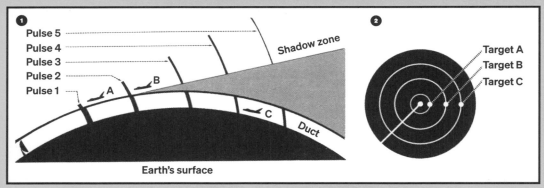

❶ Temperature inversions, in which a cold air mass is overlaid by a warmer air mass, can greatly increase the distance from which normal radar returns are received. Thus, objects appear to be much closer than they actually are, and these distant objects – superimposed on the normal radarscope picture – may result in misinterpretation and confusion

❷ The radarscope will show Targets A and B at normal range, but distant Target C will appear to be at much closer range than it actually is

4. Alien Invasion

majority of UFOs could be explained by atmospheric phenomena, or were misidentifications of ordinary things. Frequently tasked with identifying flying objects, the US Air Force created this guide to help investigators understand the effects that were known to create false UFO sightings.

This included information on both visual perception of unexplained craft and radar returns. The report explains how various aspects of human vision can potentially be tricked into seeing something that is not there.

Visual perception: How to see

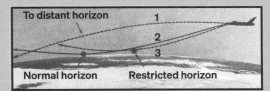

❶ Depth perception from refractive effects, caused by temperature inversion (1), normal conditions (2) and extremely warm surface air (3)

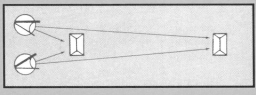

❷ Depth perception from binocular vision

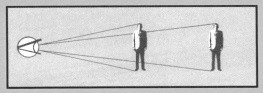

❸ Depth perception from the known size of an object and how much of our visual field it fills

❹ Depth perception from our knowledge of perspective and the convergence of parallel lines at a great distance

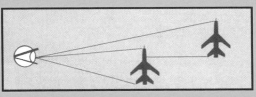

❺ Depth perception from overlapping – an object overlapped by another is known to be farther away

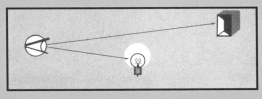

❻ Depth perception from light and shadow – an object casts a shadow away from the observer if the light is nearer

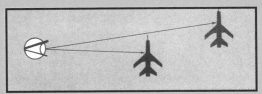

❼ Depth perception from an aerial perspective – large objects seen indistinctly apparently have haze, fog or smoke between them and the observer and, therefore, are usually at a great distance

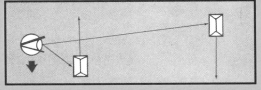

❽ Depth perception from motion parallax – when the observer fixes their sight on one object while their head or body moves, other objects apparently moving in the same direction as the observer are judged to be more distant, while those apparently moving in the opposite direction are judged to be nearer

UFO and alien sightings reported in amateur zines, 1992–97

Several hundred UFO and alien contact newsletters were published around the world between the 1950s and the 1990s. These publications, often amateur in nature, catered to a small but captivated readership, who found in them stories and theories

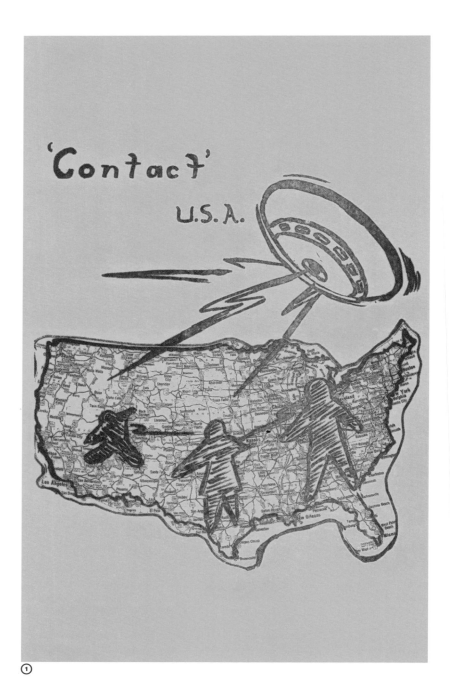

① *Contact*, No. 5, USA, 1992, front cover.

❶ *Awareness*, UK, 1992. The alien life form: self-portrait (as obtained by needle movements)
❷ *Contact*, No. 5, USA, 1992. Reported sighting of a Rocket Ezlan Air Force Base
❸ *Afrinews*, 1997. Artist's impression of an alien sighting in a homeowner's backyard, Daw Park, Adelaide, South Australia, 2.00 am, 30 May 1976 ❹ *Awareness*, 1992. Complex pictogram in wheat field. Harrow Farm, West of Froxfield, Wiltshire, UK, 10 August 1992

①

that were ridiculed or ignored by the mainstream press. Such magazines were commonly produced on a shoestring budget and were often short-lived, running for only a few years. Most of those that survived the 20th century did not continue after the advent of the Internet. The majority of UFO magazines focused on sightings within a particular country or region. Today, they provide not only a vast collection of alleged sightings and witness experiences, but also a fascinating cultural insight.

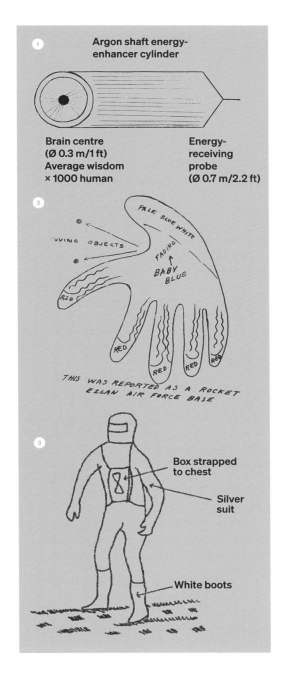

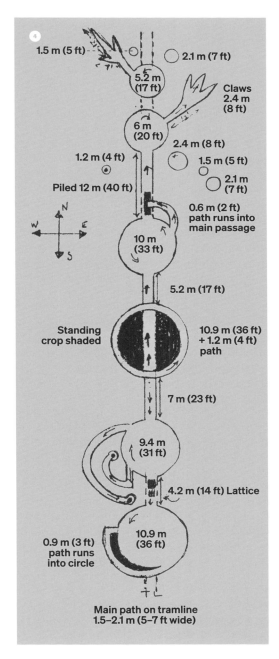

Is There Anyone Out There?

One reason aliens might visit Earth is because we have been sending them official invitations. As part of the search for extraterrestrial life (SETI), governments have sponsored transmissions to other worlds. One of the first, the 'Morse message', was broadcast by Soviet scientists in 1962. It was an early example of 'active SETI': the words '*mir*' (peace/world), 'Lenin' and 'USSR' were beamed in Morse code towards the surface of Venus. Another was sent from the Arecibo radio telescope in Puerto Rico in 1973 towards star cluster M13. Created by astronomers Frank Drake and Carl Sagan, and encoded as binary data, the Arecibo message contained information on the structure of DNA, an image of a human being and a chart showing our place in the solar system.

The US government also sent physical messages. Plaques attached to the *Pioneer* spacecraft in 1972 and 1973 showed human figures and the position of Earth relative to 14 pulsars. A similar map was etched onto a gold-plated record attached to the first *Voyager* spacecraft in 1977, together with sound recordings and images to represent humanity. In addition to the messages sent intentionally, Earth has become a giant interstellar beacon. By pumping radio and television broadcasts into the ether, humanity has advertised its existence in a way that might pique the curiosity of passing alien life.

The flipside of SETI is the search for messages – and responses – from space. Drake's Project Ozma in 1960 listened for signals on 1420 MHz – the same wavelength as radiation emitted by hydrogen – in the belief that this might be an interstellar standard. In 1971, NASA designed Project Cyclops, a SETI programme that was to involve hundreds of astronomers around the world; it was, however, abandoned because it was too expensive. In 1999, NASA launched the SETI@home project, which let the public donate the time their home computers would normally spend idle towards helping search for extraterrestrial signals. To date, the only strong candidate for an intelligent radio broadcast from space is the 'Wow! signal' received in 1977.

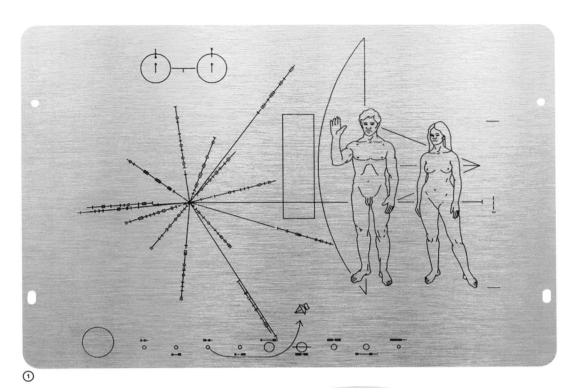

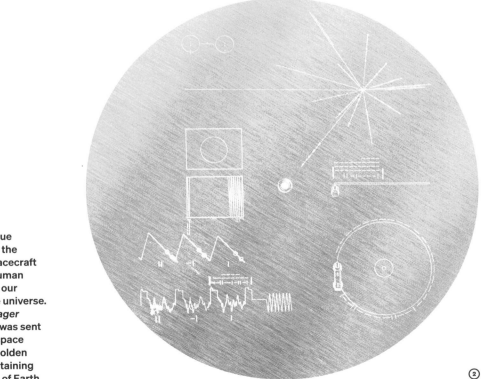

① The plaque attached to the *Pioneer* spacecraft depicted human beings and our place in the universe. ② The *Voyager* spacecraft was sent into outer space bearing a golden record, containing the sounds of Earth.

Is There Anyone Out There?

Concepts for Detection of Extraterrestrial Life, NASA, USA, 1964

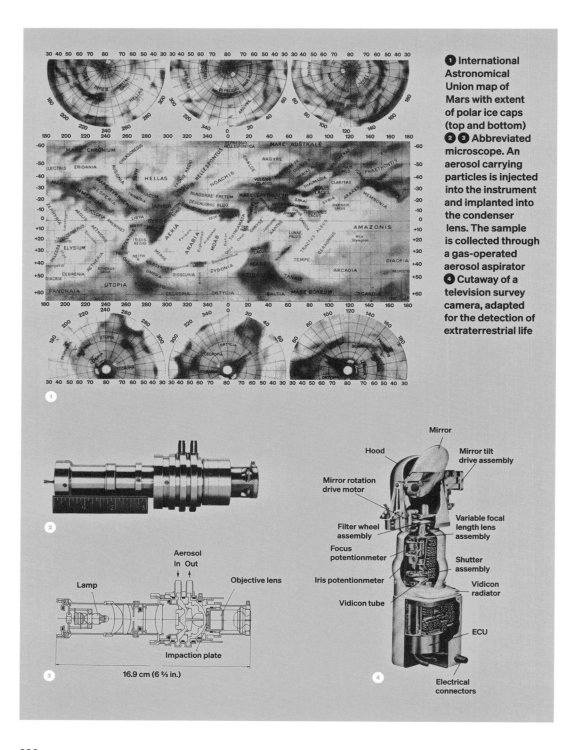

1 International Astronomical Union map of Mars with extent of polar ice caps (top and bottom)

2 3 Abbreviated microscope. An aerosol carrying particles is injected into the instrument and implanted into the condenser lens. The sample is collected through a gas-operated aerosol aspirator

4 Cutaway of a television survey camera, adapted for the detection of extraterrestrial life

Labels (figure 3): Lamp / Aerosol In Out / Objective lens / Impaction plate / 16.9 cm (6 ⅔ in.)

Labels (figure 4): Mirror / Hood / Mirror tilt drive assembly / Mirror rotation drive motor / Variable focal length lens assembly / Filter wheel assembly / Focus potentionmeter / Shutter assembly / Iris potentionmeter / Vidicon radiator / Vidicon tube / ECU / Electrical connectors

This NASA guide suggests technologies that could be used to discover evidence of life on other worlds. NASA hoped to implement a variety of detectors and microscopes in order to find tiny 'biologically significant molecules', as opposed to the walking, talking, probing humanoids that dominate cultural representations of aliens. It was thought that eventually television cameras would relay pictures back from other worlds, looking for 'foliage – and, who knows, footprints?'

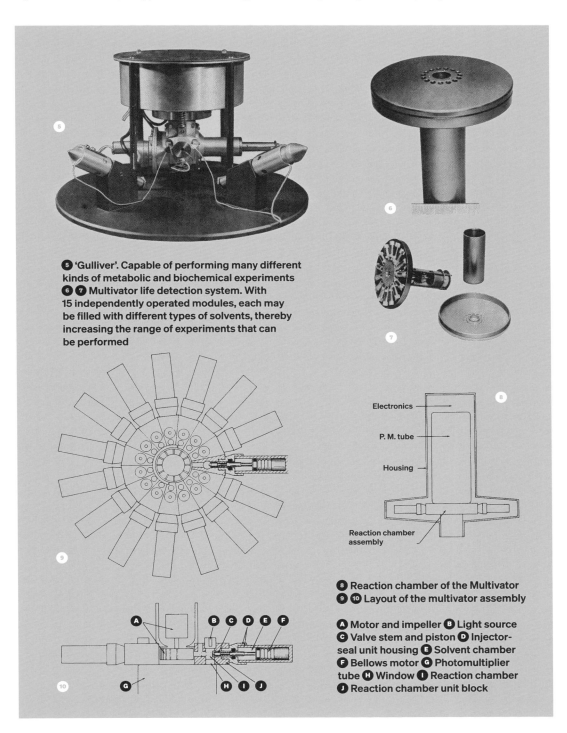

⑤ 'Gulliver'. Capable of performing many different kinds of metabolic and biochemical experiments **⑥ ⑦** Multivator life detection system. With 15 independently operated modules, each may be filled with different types of solvents, thereby increasing the range of experiments that can be performed

Electronics

P. M. tube

Housing

Reaction chamber assembly

⑧ Reaction chamber of the Multivator
⑨ ⑩ Layout of the multivator assembly

Ⓐ Motor and impeller **Ⓑ** Light source **Ⓒ** Valve stem and piston **Ⓓ** Injector-seal unit housing **Ⓔ** Solvent chamber **Ⓕ** Bellows motor **Ⓖ** Photomultiplier tube **Ⓗ** Window **Ⓘ** Reaction chamber **Ⓙ** Reaction chamber unit block

Is There Anyone Out There?

Project Cyclops: A Design Study of a System for Detecting Extraterrestrial Intelligent Life, Stanford/NASA/AMES Research Centre, USA, 1971

NASA designed Project Cyclops to coordinate the use of multiple radio telescopes to find signals from alien worlds. Although the project was shelved, the research formed the foundations of subsequent projects. These illustrations were published in *Project Cyclops: A Design Study of a System for Detecting Extraterrestrial Intelligent Life* (1971).

①

① Artist's concept of a high aerial view of the entire Cyclops system. The diameter of antenna array is about 16 km (10 mi).
② Artist's concept of a low aerial view of a portion of the Cyclops system antenna array, showing the central control and processing building.
③ Graphs and tables from Project Cyclops research.

②

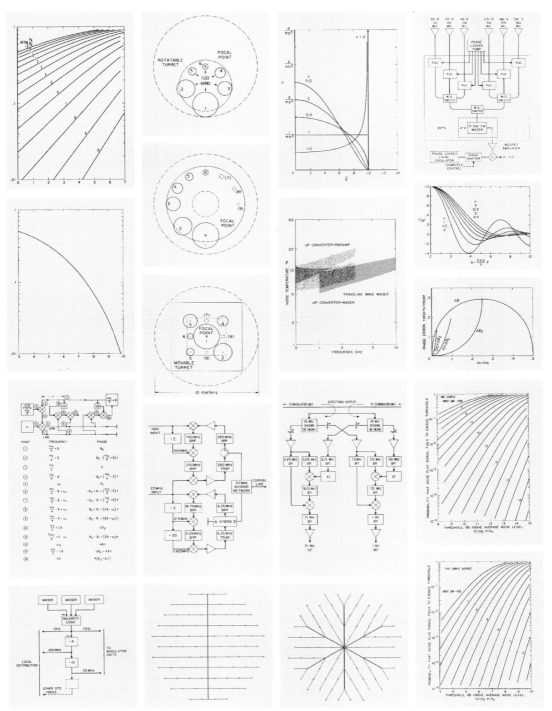

What Is the Truth?

It is safe to presume that any civilization that is capable of interstellar travel would make a formidable enemy. Consequently, it would be in humanity's best interests to get off on the right foot with any alien visitors. Any government faced with the prospect of aliens arriving on their doorstep would, therefore, need a plan of action to greet the beings without immediately offending or upsetting them. There would also need to be broad international agreement on how to treat the new arrivals. With this in mind, physicists J. Robert Oppenheimer and Albert Einstein allegedly wrote to President Harry S. Truman in 1947 to set out their views on first contact. The memo, titled 'Relationships with inhabitants of celestial bodies', also considered the position of international law as it relates to extraterrestrial entities. However, the document is of dubious provenance, riddled with spelling errors and most likely a later hoax.

Another set of supposedly genuine government documents, sent to a UFO researcher in 1984, claimed to reveal the existence of a shadowy organization called Majestic-12. The papers alleged that a secret committee within the US government had authorized plans for taking advantage of technology recovered from the incident at Roswell in 1947, in which a military weather balloon crashed. This was initially dismissed as a hoax, but researchers later found a memo in the US National Archives that appeared to support the documents' authenticity. The incident became the subject of a real FBI investigation, which determined that the original documents were bogus and that the supportive memo had been deliberately planted in the archives by hoaxers. Naturally, for those who believe in the truth of Majestic-12, the FBI investigation was simply part of a wider cover-up.

① ② ③ ④ The so-called Majestic-12 documents purport to reveal part of a conspiracy to cover up the US government's knowledge of – and interaction with – alien life. This includes the alleged recovery of a crashed UFO and alien beings at Roswell in 1947. Unusually, the FBI investigated the documents in 1988 and declared them to be 'bogus'. However, a section of the UFO community remains convinced that the documents are real.

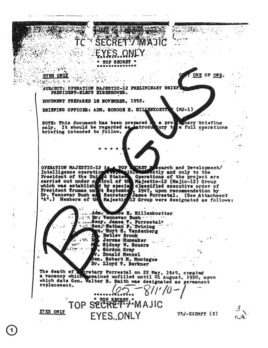

①

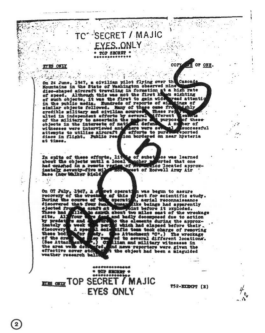

②

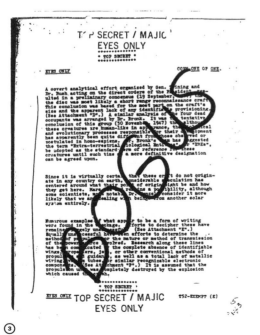

③

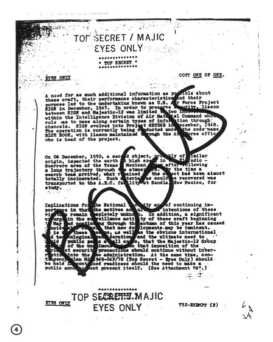

④

It is, of course, worth mentioning that 'UFO' is a loaded term. It does not, in itself, imply the presence of aliens: it simply means something in the air that is yet to be identified. In this sense, governments investigated sightings of unidentified aerial phenomena throughout the 20th century. The hardening of the Cold War threat and the descent of the Iron Curtain meant that any unusual or unexplained aerial activity had to be taken very seriously. In the years following Roswell, the number of sightings around the world grew. Worldwide saucer fever was sufficient to move UK Prime Minister Winston Churchill to write a memo to his Secretary of State for Air asking: 'What does all of this flying saucer stuff amount to? What is the truth?'

Throughout the second half of the 20th century, official projects, some of which were lengthy and wide-ranging, were commissioned to try to get to the bottom of the mystery. In the United States, Project Blue Book analysed thousands of reports to determine whether UFOs posed a realistic threat to national security. In 1969, after nearly 18 years of work, officials concluded that there was no evidence that the craft were dangerous, or that they were extraterrestrial in origin. Similar investigations are believed to have been carried out in the Soviet Union. Smaller scale enquiries have taken place in many countries, including Canada, Brazil and Italy. In France, a unit of the country's space agency known as GEIPAN has handled UFO reports since 1977. Perhaps most surprisingly, the UK government secretly conducted its own research into reports of UFO sightings as late as 1997, under the name Project Condign. The *Condign Report,* completed in 2000 and made public following a Freedom of Information request, found that the phenomenon did not pose a threat to national security. It further theorized that the sightings that could not be explained were likely the result of yet-to-be-understood atmospheric conditions.

For those who believe in alien beings, such reports are simply part of the cover-up. But what if governments were fuelling the phenomenon? One conspiracy theory flips the narrative on its head. It says that, rather than covering up real incidents, governments have deliberately encouraged the spread of stories of alien visitation and have even funded UFO research. While this may seem counterintuitive, the spread of disinformation to the public would provide the ideal cover for secret military projects, such as stealth aircraft.

Although the arrival of extraterrestrials would change everything, the fact remains that the chances of such an incident are infinitesimally small. We will likely never know to what extent governments have considered the alien threat. It seems likely, though, that they are far more preoccupied with matters here on Earth.

⑤ These photographs of fragments of an
alleged 'vehicle that travelled in outer space'
were taken by the Canadian government in 1968.

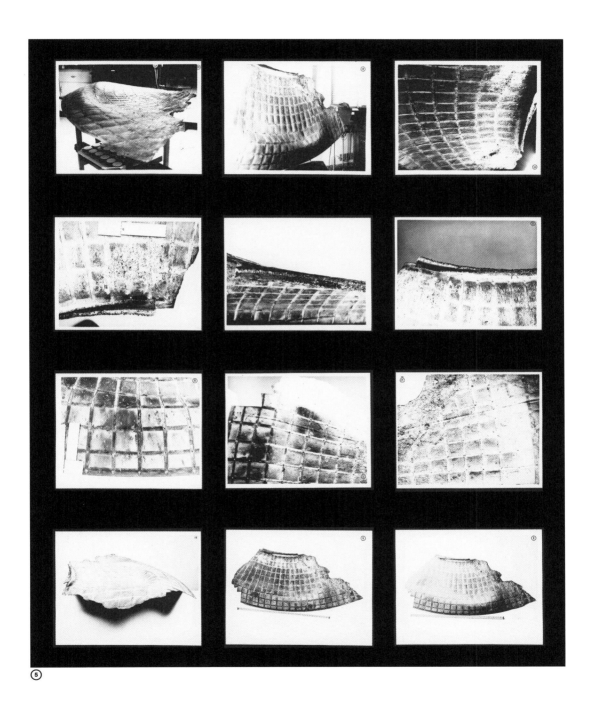

⑤

Unidentified Flying Objects Files, Defence Force, New Zealand, 1959–83 (below), 1981–84 (opposite)

New Zealand's UFO desk was kept busy with reports of flying saucers and alien encounters throughout the second half of the 20th century. Among the many documents they retained, the annotated chart of 'hard-core UFOs' may have helped keep

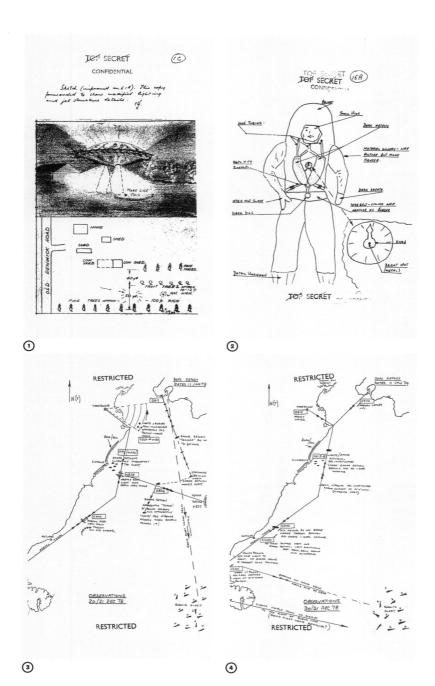

① ② ③ ④

① Sketch and map of sighting made at Old Renwick Road, Blenheim, New Zealand, 13 July 1959. ② Illustration of a being sighted within UFO at Old Renwick Road, Blenheim, New Zealand, 13 July 1959. The beings were described as 'encased in silvery shiny suits from the waist upwards when they were sitting. Their headgear seemed to be like divers' helmets, which glittered very brightly. They appeared to be normal-sized people. One of the men never moved at all. I could not see that they were carrying on any conversation at all.' ③ Map of sighting made on the night of 20/21 December 1978, on South Island, New Zealand. ④ Map of sighting made on the night of 30/31 December 1978, on South Island, New Zealand.

tabs on the types of craft spotted. Some witnesses plotted the paths of their objects on maps, while others went further and submitted detailed drawings showing the spaceships they saw (and, occasionally, their inhabitants). While those charged with replying to UFO reports usually tried to provide an explanation for each sighting, it is clear from the archives that some of their more frequent and fervent correspondents tested the patience and professionalism of the officials behind the desk.

Hard-core UFOs

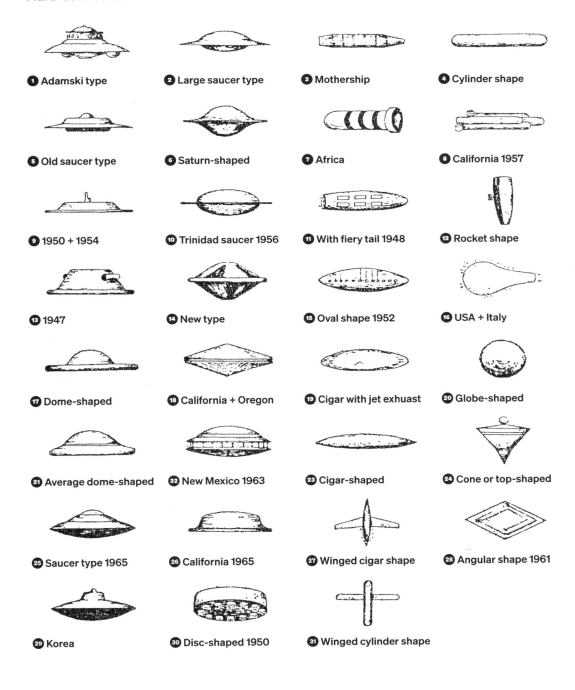

① Adamski type

② Large saucer type

③ Mothership

④ Cylinder shape

⑤ Old saucer type

⑥ Saturn-shaped

⑦ Africa

⑧ California 1957

⑨ 1950 + 1954

⑩ Trinidad saucer 1956

⑪ With fiery tail 1948

⑫ Rocket shape

⑬ 1947

⑭ New type

⑮ Oval shape 1952

⑯ USA + Italy

⑰ Dome-shaped

⑱ California + Oregon

⑲ Cigar with jet exhuast

⑳ Globe-shaped

㉑ Average dome-shaped

㉒ New Mexico 1963

㉓ Cigar-shaped

㉔ Cone or top-shaped

㉕ Saucer type 1965

㉖ California 1965

㉗ Winged cigar shape

㉘ Angular shape 1961

㉙ Korea

㉚ Disc-shaped 1950

㉛ Winged cylinder shape

Danish authorities systematically collected and investigated UFO reports made by members of the public. They provided witnesses with specially prepared report forms, which helped to ensure every detail of each sighting would be collected in a consistent way.

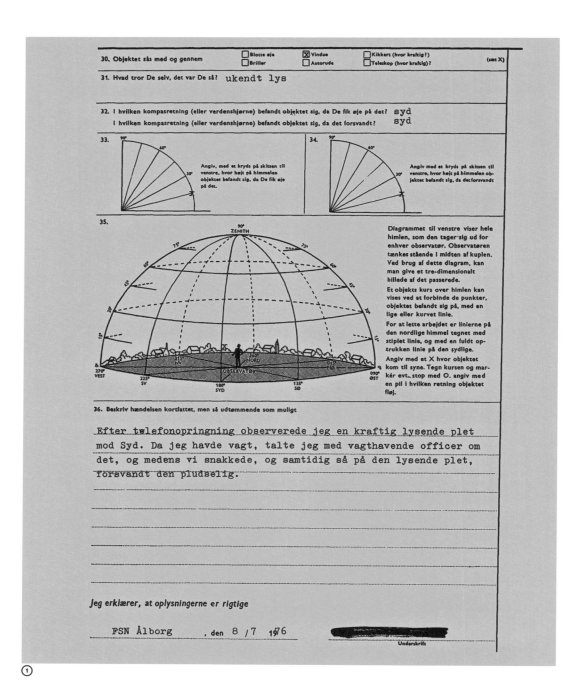

30. Objektet sås med og gennem   ☐ Blotte øje   ☒ Vindue   ☐ Kikkert (hvor kraftig?)   ☐ Briller   ☐ Autorude   ☐ Teleskop (hvor kraftig)?   (sæt X)

31. Hvad tror De selv, det var De så?   ukendt lys

32. I hvilken kompasretning (eller verdenshjørne) befandt objektet sig, da De fik øje på det?   syd
I hvilken kompasretning (eller verdenshjørne) befandt objektet sig, da det forsvandt?   syd

33.   Angiv, med et kryds på skitsen til venstre, hvor højt på himmelen objektet befandt sig, da De fik øje på det.

34.   Angiv med et kryds på skitsen til venstre, hvor højt på himmelen objektet befandt sig, da det forsvandt

35.   Diagrammet til venstre viser hele himlen, som den tager sig ud for enhver observatør. Observatøren tænkes stående i midten af kuplen. Ved brug af dette diagram, kan man give et tre-dimensionalt billede af det passerede.
Et objekts kurs over himlen kan vises ved at forbinde de punkter, objektet befandt sig på, med en lige eller kurvet linie.
For at lette arbejdet er linierne på den nordlige himmel tegnet med stiplet linie, og med en fuldt optrukken linie på den sydlige.
Angiv med et X hvor objektet kom til syne. Tegn kursen og markér evt. stop med O. angiv med en pil i hvilken retning objektet fløj.

36. Beskriv hændelsen kortfattet, men så udtømmende som muligt

Efter telefonopringning observerede jeg en kraftig lysende plet mod Syd. Da jeg havde vagt, talte jeg med vagthavende officer om det, og medens vi snakkede, og samtidig så på den lysende plet, forsvandt den pludselig.

Jeg erklærer, at oplysningerne er rigtige

FSN Ålborg   , den 8 / 7 1976   Underskrift

①

① Example of a sighting report form, including a diagram used to show the course of the UFO, as perceived by the viewer. Reporters were instructed to indicate with an 'X' where the object appeared, and then draw its course across the sky, including an arrow to indicate the direction of travel. ② Illustration of the flight of a UFO sighted on 29 October 1983, behind a house on Søndre Ringvej, 4000 Roskilde, Denmark.

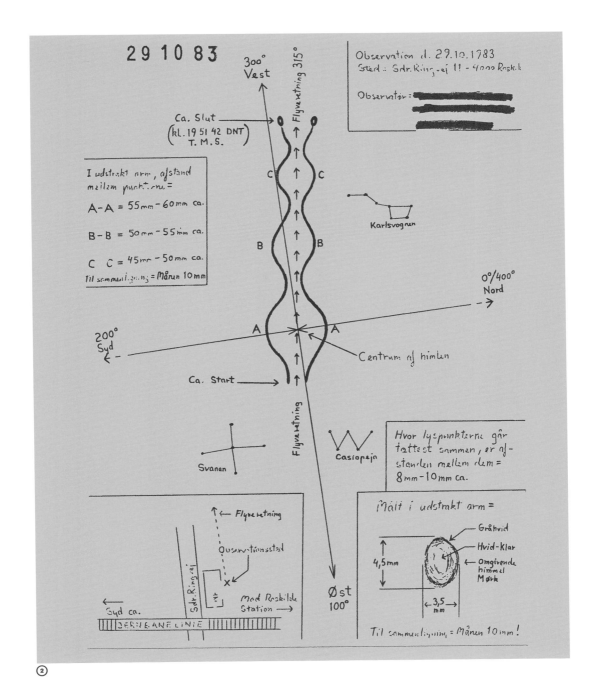

②

Unidentified Aerial Phenomena (UAP) in the UK Air Defence Region, Ministry of Defence, UK, 2000

This report was published by Project Condign, which brought together data from many thousands of sightings to determine whether UAP posed a material threat to UK interests. It suggested that more extreme experiences could be caused by some kind of field emanating from plasmas, which directly affected witnesses' brain function.

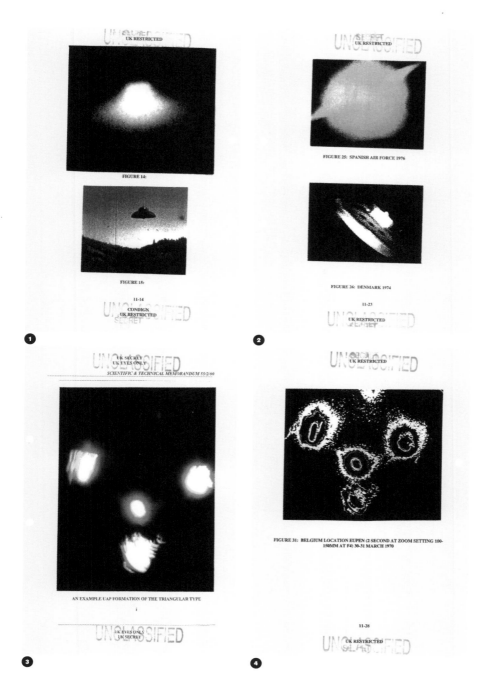

Reported sightings: ❶ Discs. Only circular in plan and thus... the same events are described by other witnesses as 'balls' or spheres ❷ Spanish Air Force, 1976 (above) and Denmark, 1974 (below) ❸ An example UAP formation of the triangular type ❹ Belgium, Location Eupen (2 second at zoom setting 100–150 mm at F4), 30–31 March 1970

Phenomena mistaken for UFOs: ❺ Lenticular cloud (above and below) ❻ Rotor cloud, UK (above) and mother of pearl (below) ❼ Seven solar images from ice crystal (above) and sun pillar and sun dog (R. Greenler) (below) ❽ Multiple light pillar display (W. Tape) (above) and light pillar (P. Parviainen) (below)

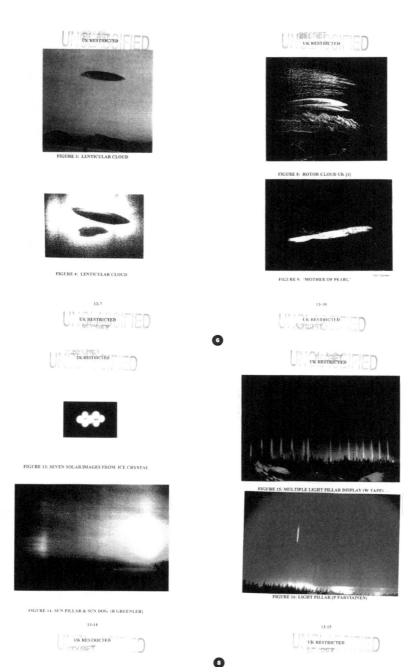

FIGURE 3: LENTICULAR CLOUD

FIGURE 4: LENTICULAR CLOUD

FIGURE 8: ROTOR CLOUD UK [1]

FIGURE 9: 'MOTHER OF PEARL'

FIGURE 13: SEVEN SOLAR IMAGES FROM ICE CRYSTAL

FIGURE 14: SUN PILLAR & SUN DOG (R GREENLER)

FIGURE 15: MULTIPLE LIGHT PILLAR DISPLAY (W TAPE)

FIGURE 16: LIGHT PILLAR (P PARVIAINEN)

Resources

Manuals Featured Within This Book

Advanced Spotters' Field Guide (USA: US Department of Commerce, 1993), see pages 100–1

Advising the Householder (UK: Home Office, 1963), see pages 168–69

Aids to Identification of Flying Objects (USA: Air Force, 1968), see pages 230–31

Arctic Survival (UK: Air Ministry, 1953), see pages 148–49

Army: Survive to Fight (UK: Director of Army Training, 1983), see pages 212–13

Bás/Beatha (Death/Life) (Ireland: Department of Defence, 1965), see pages 206–7

Civil Defence (Zivilschutzfibel) (West Germany: Federal Office for the Civil Protection of Bad Godesberg, 1964), see pages 170–71

Civil Defence (Гражданская оборона) (Soviet Union: 1986) see pages 98, 114–15, 136–37, 214–15

Civil Defence Manual of Basic Training: Basic Chemical Warfare (UK: Home Office, 1949), see pages 188–91

Concepts for Detection of Extraterrestrial Life (USA: NASA, 1964), see pages 236–37

Danger: Your Safety? Hazards in Yellowstone National Park (USA: US Government Printing Office, 1975 and 1983), see page 107

Disaster Preparedness Tokyo (東京防災) (Japan: Tokyo Metropolitan Government, 2015), see pages 122–23

Domestic Nuclear Shelters (UK: Home Office, 1981), see pages 184–85

Earthquakes and Preparedness: Before, During and After (USA: Earthquake Preparedness Society, 1989), see pages 116–19

Education for National Survival (USA: Department of Health, Education and Welfare, 1956), see pages 192–93

11 Steps to Survival (Canada: Emergency Measures Organization, 1961), see pages 200–1

Facts About Unidentified Flying Objects (USA: Library of Congress Legislative Reference Service, 1966), see pages 228–29

Fallout on the Farm (Canada: Department of Agriculture, 1961), see page 199

Fallout Protection (USA: Office of Civil Defence, 1961), see pages 182–83

Family Earthquake Safety: Home Hazard Hunt and Drill (USA: Federal Emergency Management Agency, 1986), see pages 112–13

The Family Fallout Shelter (USA: Office of Civil and Defence Mobilization, 1959) see pages 176–77

Flood Damage Reduction Manual (USA: US Army Corps of Engineers, 1984), see pages 96–97

Forest Fires: How to Fight Them (USA: Commonwealth of Pennsylvania Department of Forestry, 1922), see pages 130–31

Home Defence and the Farmer (UK: Ministry of Agriculture, Fisheries and Food, 1958), see page 198

Home Protection Exercises (USA: Federal Civil Defence Administration, 1953), see pages 166–67

The Hydrogen Bomb (UK: Home Office, 1957), see pages 194–95

In the Time of Emergency (USA: Office of Civil Defence, 1968), see pages 86–88

Jungle Survival (UK: Air Ministry, 1950), see pages 144–47

Know to Live (Savoir pour vivre) (France: National Service for Civil Protection, 1960, see pages 178–79

Learning to Live in Earthquake Country: Preparedness for People with Disabilities (USA: Federal Emergency Management Agency, 1984), see pages 110–11

Live: Three Plans for Survival in Nuclear Attack (USA: Stanford Research Institute, 1960), see pages 154, 180–81

Manual: Forest Fire Fighters Service (USA: Minnesota Office of Civilian Defence, 1942), see pages 132–33

Personal Protection Under Atomic Attack (Canada: Civil Defence Canada, 1951), see pages 8–17

Project Cyclops: A Design Study of a System for Detecting Extraterrestrial Intelligent Life (USA: Stanford/NASA/AMES Research Centre, 1971), see pages 238–39

Protect and Survive (UK: Home Office, 1980), see pages 210–11

Spanish Influenza (Australia: Board of Public Health, 1918), see page 52

Survival in Likely Target Areas (Canada: Emergency Measures Organization, 1962), see pages 202–5

Surviving Doomsday, Colin Bruce Sibley (UK: Shaw & Sons, 1977), see pages 208–9

The Thames Barrier (UK: Greater London Council, 1980s), see page 99

Timely Tips When Disaster Strikes, Judge Sherman G. Finesilver (USA: Howard Warren, 1969), see page 89

Tornado (USA: US Department of Commerce, 1973), see pages 90–93

Twister! Tornado Tips to Save Your Life (USA: Illinois Emergency Services and Disaster Agency, 1983), see pages 94–95

The UFO Evidence (USA: National Investigations Committee on Aerial Phenomena (NICAP), 1964), see pages 226–27

UFO Sighting Reports (Denmark: Air Force, 1976–2002), see pages 246–47

Unidentified Aerial Phenomena (UAP) in the UK Air Defence Region (UK: Ministry of Defence, 2000), see pages 248–49

Unidentified Flying Objects Files (New Zealand: Defence Force, 1959–83 and 1981–84), see pages 244–45

US Air Force Survival School (USA: Department of the Air Force, 1985), see pages 150–51

Volcanoes (Mexico: Secretary of Security and Citizen Protection, 2021), see pages 124–25

What to Do... (Co dělat...) (Czechoslovakia: Federal Ministry of the Interior, 1972), see pages 172–73

Wildland Fire Suppression Tactics Reference Guide (USA: National Wildfire Coordinating Group, 1996), see pages 138–39

Yogi, the Be-Prepared Bear: Earthquake Preparedness for Children (USA: Hanna-Barbera Productions, 1984), see page 104

Further Reading

Alexis-Martin, Becky, *Disarming Doomsday: The Human Impact of Nuclear Weapons Since Hiroshima* (London: Pluto Press, 2019)

Barry, John M., *The Great Influenza: The Story of the Deadliest Pandemic in History* (London: Penguin, 2020)

Clarke, David, *The UFO Files: The Inside Story of Real-life Sightings* (London: Bloomsbury, 2012)

Davis, Tracy C., *Stages of Emergency: Cold War Nuclear Civil Defence* (Durham, NC: Duke University Press, 2007)

Ellsberg, Daniel, *The Doomsday Machine: Confessions of a Nuclear War Planner* (London: Bloomsbury, 2017)

Evans, Hilary and Dennis Stacy (eds.), *UFO 1947–1997: Fifty Years of Flying Saucers* (London: John Brown, 1997)

Freedman, Norman, *The Cold War: Threat, Paranoia and Oppression* (Eustis, FL: Seven Oaks, 2019)

Gorightly, Adam, *Saucers, Spooks and Kooks: UFO Disinformation in the Age of Aquarius* (USA: Daily Grail Publishing, 2021)

Honigsbaum, Mark, *The Pandemic Century: A History of Global Contagion from the Spanish Flu to Covid-19* (London: W. H. Allen, 2020)

Huyghe, Patrick, *The Field Guide to Extraterrestrials* (London: New English Library, 1997)

Keel, John, *Operation Trojan Horse* (New York, NY: Putnam, 1970)

Keller, Edward A. and Duane E. DeVecchio, *Natural Hazards: Earth's Processes as Hazards, Disasters, and Catastrophes* (Upper Saddle River, NJ: Pearson, 2006)

Musson, Roger, *The Million Death Quake: The Science of Predicting Earth's Deadliest Natural Disaster* (Basingstoke: Macmillan, 2012)

Pilkington, Mark, *Mirage Men: A Journey into Disinformation, Paranoia and UFOs* (London: Constable, 2010)

Quick, Jonathan D., *The End of Epidemics: How to Stop Viruses and Save Humanity Now* (Melbourne; London: Scribe, 2018)

Schlosser, Eric, *Command and Control* (London: Allen Lane, 2009)

Schneider, Bonnie, *Extreme Weather: A Guide to Surviving Flash Floods, Tornadoes, Hurricanes, Heat Waves, Snowstorms, Tsunamis, and Other Natural Disasters* (New York, NY: Macmillan, 2012)

Sherman, Irwin, *Twelve Diseases that Changed Our World* (Washington DC: ASM Press, 2007)

Shilts, Randy, *And the Band Played On: Politics, People, and the AIDS Epidemic* (New York, NY: St Martin's Press, 1987)

Spinney, Laura, *Pale Rider: The Spanish Flu of 1918 and How it Changed the World* (New York, NY: Public Affairs, 2017)

Valée, Jacques, *Passport to Magonia: From Folklore to Flying Saucers* (USA: Daily Grail Publishing, 2014)

Westad, Odd Arne, *The Cold War: A World History* (London: Penguin, 2017)

Young, Taras, *Nuclear War in the UK* (London: Four Corners Books, 2019)

Sources

Every effort has been made to locate and credit copyright holders of the material reproduced in this book. The author and publisher apologize for any omissions or errors, which can be corrected in future editions.

a= above, **b**=below, **l**=left, **r**=right, **c**=centre

2, Shaw & Sons, **4**, *Zivilschutzfibel* (Federal Minister of the Federal Office for the Civil Protection of Bad Godesberg, 1964), **4**, Courtesy of the National Library of Medicine, **7**, Photo 12 / Alamy Stock Photo, **8–17**, *Personal Protection Under Atomic Attack* (1951), Health Canada, **19**, Allstar Picture Library Ltd. / Alamy Stock Photo, **20**, Courtesy of the National Library of Medicine, **22**, © Zwerdling Nursing Archives, Courtesy of the National Library of Medicine, **25**, Samuel D. Erhart, 'The Trailing Skirt: Death Loves a Shining Mark', *Puck* (1900), **27**, Library of Congress Prints and Photographs Division Washington, D.C. , **29al, ar, bc, br,** Courtesy of the National Library of Medicine, **29bl**, © Zwerdling Nursing Archives, Courtesy of the National Library of Medicine, **30–31**, Courtesy of the National Library of Medicine, used by permission of the American Lung Association, Lung.org., **32–33**, Courtesy of the National Library of Medicine and the Rockefeller Archive Centre, **34–35**, Otto and Marie Neurath Isotype Collection, University of Reading, **36–37**, Courtesy of the National Library of Medicine, **38–41**, Courtesy of the National Library of Medicine, **42**, Christian Medical College in Vellore, courtesy of the National Library of Medicine, **43**, National Tuberculosis Institute in India, courtesy of the National Library of Medicine, **45a**, US National Archives, 45499309, **45bl**, Underwood Archives via Getty Images, **45br**, US National Archives, 26428662, **47a**, Patterson, K. David and Gerald F. Pyle. "The Geography and Mortality of the 1918 Influenza Pandemic." Bulletin of the History of Medicine 65:1 (1991), 12, Fig. 5. © 1991 Johns Hopkins University Press. Reprinted with permission of Johns Hopkins University Press., **47bl**, Sanitation, Influenza, Mortality Deaths in U.S. Cities (Chart)' (Reeve 2721). OHA 80 Reeve Photograph Collection. Otis Historical Archives, National Museum of Health and Medicine, **47br**, Sanitation, Excess Mortality in U.S. Cities During Influenza Epidemic, 1918-19 (Chart)' (Reeve 3141). OHA 80 Reeve Photograph Collection. Otis Historical Archives, National Museum of Health and Medicine, **48a**, Virginia Commonwealth University Libraries, **48c**, Staatsarchiv Basel-Stadt, Sanität Q 3.3, **48b**, Municipal Library, City of New York, **49l**, Municipal Library, City of New York, **49r**, Photo A13187 appears courtesy of the Provincial Archives of Alberta, **50–51**, 'Modern Japanese Translation: Influenza', translated by Shuichi Nishimura: Heibonsha Limited Publishers, 2021 **52**, Oliver Wade, Spanish Influenza: All About It, 1919, **53**, Courtesy of the National Library of Medicine, **54a**, The Asahi Shimbun via Getty Images, **54c**, Bettmann via Getty Images, **54bl**, Hulton Deutsch via Getty Images, **54br**, Bettmann via Getty Images, **57a**, Daily Herald Archive via Getty Images, **57bl**, Bridgeman Images, **57br**, Bettmann via Getty Images, **58al**, Shawshots / Alamy Stock Photo, **58ar**, Mistol Mist advertisement, David M. Rubenstein Rare Book & Manuscript Library, Duke University, **58b**, Public domain, **59**, Courtesy of the National Library of Medicine, **61a**, Jaime Razuri via Getty Images, **61cl**, Fairfax Media Archives via Getty Images, **61cr**, San Francisco Chronicle/Hearst Newspapers via Getty Images, **61b**, Valerie Winckler via Getty Images, **62al**, Superman disguised as 'bleachman' wearing a condom as a hat; instruction leaflet on how to clean syringes issued by the San Francisco AIDS Foundation. Colour lithograph, 1988. Wellcome Collection, **62ar**, The black and white figures of a couple hugging within a border decorated with the national colours of Zimbabwe. Colour lithograph by J. Shepherd for the AIDS Counselling Trust (ACT) of Zimbabwe, 1991. Wellcome Collection, **62bl**, Condoman says: don't be shame be game : use condoms!. Wellcome Collection, **62br**, Copyright 2022 New York City Department of Health and Mental Hygiene. Reprinted with permission., **64**, Illustrations and text explaining how to live positively with AIDS; including getting medical help when you feel unwell to not getting pregnant; one of a series of educational posters issued by the Committed Communities Development Trust in Mumbai. Colour lithograph, ca. 1997. Wellcome Collection, **65**, A man wearing the same red striped shirt in numerous public engagements relating to public hygiene including swimming and standing on a crowded bus representing an advertisement for ways in which you cannot contract AIDS; a poster sponsored by Unicef. Colour lithograph by Adprint, ca. 1997. Wellcome Collection, **67a**, Russian Defence Ministry via Getty Images, **67c**, Hindustan Times via Getty Images, **67bl**, Prakash Singh via Getty Images, **67br**, Franco Origlia via Getty Images, **70**, National Health Service, Open Government Licence v3.0 (OGL v3), **71**, World Health Organization, **72**, National Health Service, Open Government Licence v3.0 (OGL v3), **73al**, Stas Tuchinsky, **73acl**, Giovana Romano, **73acr**, Irene Martinez, Try Your Best Not To Stress, Poster design, Valencia, 2020, **73ar** Birute Kotryna, **73cl**, Oliver Klughardt, **73ccl**, Staying Home is Staying Safe by Manuella Martins, 2020. São Paulo, Brazil. www.manuellamartins.com, **73ccr**, El Sheikha, Nour. Digital Poster 2020 **73cr**, Kyra Erin Hirson, @astro. illustrations, **73bl**, Elisa Bedcuts, **73bcl**, © JAZZ HANDS / Yannick Van Houtven, **73bcr**, Xu Kai, **73br**, Mustafa Akman, **74**, *Savoir Pour Vivre* (1955), Ministère de l'intérieur, Service national de la protection civile, **76**, Heritage Auctions, HA.com, **79**, David Rumsey Map Collection. www.davidrumsey.com, **80**, Extinction Rebellion, **83a**, Granger/Shutterstock, **83cl, bl**, Library of Congress Prints and Photographs Division Washington, D.C. , **83cr**, Bettmann via Getty Images, **83br**, Buyenlarge via Getty Images, **84a**, Buyenlarge via Getty Images, **84cl**, Ullstein bild Dtl. via Getty Images, **84cr**, University of Southern California via Getty Images, **84b**, Mirrorpix via Getty Images, **86–88**, *In Time of*

Emergency (1968), **89**, The Denver Public Library, Western History Collection, [Call 574767]., **91–93**, *Tornado: US Department of Commerce* (1973), **94–95**, *Twister! Tornado Tips to Save Your Life* (1983), **96–97**, *Flood Damage Reduction Manual* (1984), **98**, Public domain, **99**, *GLC Thames Barrier, Flood Defence for London* (1980s), Greater London Council, **100–1**, *Advanced Spotters' Field Guide* (1993), **103a**, US National Archives, 2127357, **103c**, US National Archives, 2127302, **103bl**, Library of Congress Prints and Photographs Division Washington, D.C., **103br**, Library of Congress via Getty Images, **104**, *Yogi, the Be-Prepared Bear – Earthquake Preparedness for Children* (1984), Warner Bros, **106**, Library of Congress Prints and Photographs Division Washington, D.C., **107**, *Danger: Your Safety? Hazards in Yellowstone National Park* (1975 and 1983), **108–9**, Stefan R. Landsberger Collection, International Institute of Social History (Amsterdam), **110–11**, *Learning to Live in Earthquake Country: Preparedness for People with Disabilities* (1984), **112–13**, *Family Earthquake Safety: Home Hazard Hunt and Drill* (1986), **114–15**, Public domain, **116–19**, *Earthquakes and Preparedness Before, During, and After* (1989), **120–21**, National Emergency Management Agency (NZ), **122–23**, *Disaster Preparedness Tokyo (Tokyo Bosai)* (2015), Tokyo Metropolitan Government, **124–25**, Copyright Centro Nacional de Prevención de Desastres , **127a**, Historical via Getty Images, **127cl**, Library of Congress Prints and Photographs Division Washington, D.C. , **127cr**, Fairfax Media Archives via Getty Images, **127b**, The Sydney Morning Herald via Getty Images, **129a, bl, br**, National Archives, France (Posters announcing the fire, security and passive defense exhibitions organized by the work for security and the organization of relief, 1929–1939, 20040297/1, 20040297/2, 20040297/3), **129bc**, Archives nationales du monde du travail (Roubaix), PI 51 13, Pièces isolées iconographiques, **130–31**, Library of Congress Prints and Photographs Division Washington, D.C. , **132–33**, *Manual: Forest Fire Fighters Service* (1942), **134–35**, National Safety Council of Australia, State Library Victoria, **136–37**, Public domain, **138–39**, *Wildland Fire Suppression Tactics Reference Guide* (1996), **141a**, Harry Todd via Getty Images, **141cl**, Frederic Lewis via Getty Images, **141cr**, Ullstein bild Dtl. via Getty Images, **141b**, University of Southern California via Getty Images, **143–49**, *Arctic Survival* (1953) and *Jungle Survival* (1950), **150–51**, *US Air Force Survival School* (1985), **152**, Public domain, **154**, *Three Plans for Survival in Nuclear Attack* (1960), **157**, National Széchényi Library, Collection of Small Prints and Posters, **159**, *Nuclear Weapons, Their Effects and Your Protection* (1986), **159**, *Protect and Survive* (1980), Central Office of Information, **161**, H. Armstrong Roberts/ ClassicStock via Getty Images, **161**, *Education for National Survival* (1956), **162al**, Shutterstock, **162ar**, Historical via Getty Images, **162b**, Bettmann via Getty Images, **163**, Lawrence Schiller via Getty Images, **164–65**, National Archives Japan, **166–67**, *Home Protection Exercises* (1957), **168–69**, *Advising the Householder* (1963), **170–71**, *Zivilschutzfibel* (Federal Minister of the Federal Office for the Civil Protection of Bad Godesberg, 1964), **172–73**, Private Collection, **175a**, l, *Emergency Aid by Civil Defence* (1987), Federal Office of Civil Defence (Switzerland), **175cr**, Graham Turner / Stringer via Getty Images, **175cl**, Keystone-France via Getty Images, **175b**, John Drysdale via Getty Images, **176–77**, *Family Fallout Shelter* (1959), **178–79**, *Savoir Pour Vivre* (1955) Ministère de l'intérieur, Service national de la protection civil, **180–81**, *Three Plans for Survival in Nuclear Attack* (1960), **182–83**, *Fallout Protection* (1961), **184–85**, Domestic Nuclear Shelters (1981), **187a**, Science and Society Picture Library, **187bl**, bc, br, Historical via Getty Images, **188–91**, *Civil Defence Manual of Basic Training: Basic Chemical Warfare* (1949), **192–93**, *Education for National Survival* (1956), **194–95**, *The Hydrogen Bomb* (1957), Central Office of Information, **196–97**, *Estimated Damage Posters Before and After* (1958), HMSO, **198**, *Home Defence and the Farmer* (1958), Ministry of Agriculture, Fisheries and Food and Central Office of Information, **199**, *Fallout on the Farm* (1961), Canada Department of Agriculture, **200–1**, *11 Steps* (1961), Canada Department of National Defence, **202–5**, *Surival in Likely Target Areas* (1962), Canada Department of National Defence, **206–7**, *Bás/Beatha* (1965), Department of Defence, **208–9**, Shaw & Sons, **210–11**, *Protect and Survive* (1980), Central Office of Information, **212–13**, *Survive to Fight, Army Code No. 71338* (1983), **214–15**, Public domain, **216**, *Project Cyclops: A Design Study of a System for Detecting Extraterrestial Intelligent Life* (1971), **218**, Bettmann via Getty Images, **221a**, Granger Historical Picture Archive / Alamy Stock Photo, **221cl, cr, b**, Bettmann via Getty Images, **223al**, *INFO OVNI* (1975), **223ar**, *UFO-QUEBEC* (1976), **223bl**, *UFO Information* (1976), **223bc**, *Stendek* (1972), **223br**, *Lumières Dans la Nuit* (1968), **225a**, Library of Congress via Getty Images, **225cl, b**, Bettmann via Getty Images, **225cr**, Universal History Archive via Getty Images, **226–27**, *The UFO Evidence* (1964), NICAP, CIA-RDP81R00560R0001 00010001-0, **228–31**, Library of Congress Prints and Photographs Division Washington, D.C., **232**, *Contact* (1992), **233al, r**, *Awareness* (1992), **233cl**, *Contact*, 1992, **233bl**, *Afrinews* (1997), **235**, NASA/JPL, **236–37**, *Concepts for the Detection of Extraterrestrial Life* (1964), **238–39**, *Project Cyclops: A Design Study of a System for Detecting Extraterrestial Intelligent Life* (1971), **241**, *Operation Majestic-12*, FBI, **243**, Declassified Canadian UFO Documents, **244–45**, *Reports of UFOs [Unidentified Flying Objects]* (1981–84), Defence Force, **246–47**, Danish Defence, Flyvevåbnets UFO-arkiv, **248–49**, *Unidentified Aerial Phenomena (UAP) in the UK Air Defence Region* (2000), Ministry of Defence, **front cover**, illustration created by Daniel Streat, Visual Fields, **endpapers**, *Zivilschutzfibel* (Federal Minister of the Federal Office for the Civil Protection of Bad Godesberg, 1964)

Index

Illustrations are in **bold**.

activism **61, 80**
advertising 56, **58**
agriculture, nuclear
  fallout **198–9,
  206–7**
AIDS 6, 17, 23, 26, 31,
  60–3, **64–5**
air raid defence
  164–5
aliens *see also* UFOs
  abductions **221,** 222,
  224
  appearance 220,
  222, **244**
  detection of life 234,
  236–9
  first contact 240
  invasion 8, 219, **223,**
  224
Arctic survival 142,
  148–9
Aricibo message 234
Armero, Columbia 14
Arnold, Kenneth **221,**
  222
Asian flu 6, **54,** 55–6
Australia
  fire **127, 134–5**
  HIV/AIDS 17, **61–2**
  nuclear attack **159**
  Spanish flu 46, **52**
Avian flu 68, **69**

Baden-Powell, Robert
  142
Belgium **29**
Black Death 23
Boxing Day 2004
  tsunami 9–10
bubonic plague 23
business adaptations
  45

Calmette, Albert 28
Canada
  nuclear attack 7,
  160, 163, **199–205**
  UFOs **243**
'Catch It, Bin it, Kill it,'
  UK **70**
censorship 46

chemical warfare
  188–91
Chile 105
China
  Asian flu **54,** 55
  earthquakes **108–9**
  nuclear attack 187
  SARS-CoV-1 66
  tuberculosis (TB)
  29, **36–41**
Christmas seals 29
Churchill, Winston 242
civil defence 17, 155–9,
  160–3, **164–73,** 174,
  188–91
climate change 78–81,
  126, 128
clothing, hygiene
  concerns 25
cognitive bias 10, 14
cold remedies 56, **58**
Cold War 7, 155–6,
  158–9, 187, 242
communication
  methods 10–11
communism 16
Condign Report, UK
  242, **248–9**
consequence-based
  messaging 15
coronaviruses 66
COVID-19 9, **67,** 68, **69,**
  72–3
Cuban Missile Crisis
  7, 156
cultural identity 17–18
Czechoslovakia,
  172–3

deforestation 126
Denmark **246–7**
diagnosis,
  tuberculosis (TB)
  31
diversity 17–18
'Don't Die of Ignorance,'
  UK 23, 63
Drake, Frank 234
drought 81
drug resistance 31
drug users 60, **61**
'Duck and Cover,' USA
  11, **162**

earthquakes 18, 78,
  102, **103–4,** 105,
  108–19, 122–3
Einstein, Albert 240
Extinction Rebellion **80**

face masks **45,** 46–9,
  52–3, 57, 73
films **7,** 13–14, **19,** 219
fire **76,** 81, 126–8,
  129–39
first aid 140, **166–7, 213**
flooding 12, 14–15, 78,
  81, **84,** 85, **86, 96–9**
France
  aliens **223,** 242
  fire **129**
  HIV/AIDS 61
  nuclear attack 163,
  178–9
  Spanish flu 46
  tuberculosis (TB)
  27, 28, **29, 32–3**

Germany
  nuclear attack
  170–1, 175
  Spanish flu 46, **48**
globalization 6, 24, 66
government
  responses 9, 10, 46
Greenland 81
Guérin, Albert 28

Hajj **71**
hand hygiene **72, 73**
Hawaii 102
Heaf test 31
heatwaves 81
Hill, Betty and Barney
  221, 222
Hilleman, Maurice 56
HIV/AIDS 6, 17, 23, 26,
  31, 60–3, **64–5**
homosexuality 17, 60,
  63
Hong Kong flu 6, 17,
  54, 56
hospitals, **45**
Hungary, civil defence
  17, **157**
hurricanes 78, **79, 83,**
  89

hydrogen bomb
  194–5

ice melt 81
ideologies 15–17
India
  Asian flu 55
  COVID-19 **67**
  HIV/AIDS **64–5**
  tuberculosis (TB)
  42–3
influenza *see* Asian
  flu; Hong Kong flu;
  Spanish flu
Ireland 186, **206–7**
isotypes **34–5**
Italy
  COVID-19 **67**
  flooding **84**
  Spanish flu 46
  tornados 85
  tuberculosis (TB)
  22, 29

Japan
  air raid defence
  164–5
  Asian flu **54**
  earthquake advice
  18
  earthquakes 105,
  122–3
  flooding **84**
  Spanish flu **50–1**
  jungle survival 142,
  144–6

Kennedy, John F. 174
Koch, Robert 28

languages 18, 105
leprosy **42**
London, flooding 12,
  85, **99**

McCartney, Paul 56
Macmillan, Harold 55–6
MAD (mutually
  assured destruction)
  8, 158
Majestic-12 240, **241**
Mantoux test 31
Martinique 102–5

Mbeki, Thabo 63
Mecca **71**
MERS 68, **69, 71**
Mexico 14–15, **124–5**
migration 81
monsoons 81, 85
mortality rates
Asian flu 56
COVID-19 **69**
Hong Kong flu 56
Spanish flu **47**

NASA 234, **238–9**
nationalism 17–18, **54**
navigation **149**
Nevado del Ruiz
volcano 14
New Zealand 105,
120–1, 244–5
normalcy bias 14, 102
'Now You See It, Now
You Don't' (Shields)
219
nuclear attack
blast and fallout
186–7, **192–215**
civil defence 155–9,
160–3, **164–73**
deterrence 7–8
shelter **168**, 174,
175–85

Obama, Barack 66
Oppenheimer, J.
Robert 240

pandemic, first use
of word 24
Peru **61**
Philippines 105
Pioneer spacecraft
234, **235**
Plague of Justinian 23
Poland, Spanish flu 49
Popocatépetl, Mexico
14–15, **124**
population growth 24
prediction of natural
disasters 77–8
'preppers' 140, 142
Project Blue Book, 242
Project Cyclops 234,
238–9

propaganda 16
'Protect and Survive,'
UK 11, 16–17, 155, **159**,
186, **210–12**
public information
campaigns 10–18

quarantine 66

rafts **145**
Reagan, Ronald 60, 63
Red Cross **27, 45, 53,**
164–5
research
abstract guidance
15
government-
sponsored 7
risk perception 13–15
Roswell incident 222,
240, 242

Sagan, Carl 234
SARS-CoV-1 66, **69**
Scouts 140, **141**, 142
sea levels 81
SETI (search for extra-
terrestrial life) 234
Singapore 55, 66–8
smallpox **42**
'Smokey Bear,' USA 128
social distancing 49,
67, 73
South Africa 63
Soviet Union
earthquakes **114–15**
fire **136–7**
flooding **98**
nuclear attack 156,
160–3, 174, **214–15**
tornados 85
tuberculosis (TB) 31
UFOs 242
Spain **223**
Spanish flu 6, 44–9,
50–3, 66
spitting 28, **33, 35, 39,**
42, 43, 48, 49
storms 78, **88, 100–1,**
128
supervolcanoes 105–7
survival kit guidance
120–1, 174, **178–9**

survival skills 140–2,
143–51
Sweden **175, 223**
Swine flu 66, **69, 70**
Switzerland
nuclear attack **175**
Spanish flu 49

Thames River 12, 85, **99**
Thatcher, Margaret
16–17, 211
tornados 14, 15, 82–5,
87, 90–5, 126
Truman, Harry S. 240
trust 13, 14, 17
tsunamis 9–10, 102
tuberculosis (TB) **22,**
26–31, **32–43**

UFOs 8, **218,** 219,
220–2, **223, 225–33,**
242, **243–7**
UK
Asian flu 55–6, **57**
chemical warfare
188–91
COVID-19 **72**
flooding 12, **84,** 85,
99
HIV/AIDS 23, 60, 63
Hong Kong flu 56
nuclear attack 11,
16–17, 155, 156, **159,**
160, 163, **168–9,** 174,
175, 184–5, 186,
194–8, 208–11
survival skills **143–9**
Swine flu 66, **70**
tornados 85
tuberculosis (TB) 31
UFOs **233,** 242,
248–9
UNESCO 102
USA
Asian flu 56, **58–9**
earthquakes **103–4,**
110–13, 116–19
extraterrestrial life
detection **236–9**
fire **76, 127,** 128,
130–3, 138–9
first aid **166–7**
flooding **84, 86, 96–7**

HIV/AIDS 60, **61–2,** 63
Hong Kong flu **54,** 56
hurricanes 78, **79,**
83, 89
nuclear attack 11,
154, 160, **161–2,** 174,
176–7, 180–3, 192–3
Spanish flu 44, **45,**
46, **47–8,** 49, **53**
storms **88, 100–1**
survival skills **150–1**
tornados 82–5, **87,**
90–5
tuberculosis (TB)
29, 31, **34–5**
UFOs **218,** 220–2,
225–32, 242
Yellowstone Caldera
105–7

vaccines
Bacillus Calmette–
Guérin (BCG) 28, 31
COVID-19 9, **67**
flu 56, **57,** 66
virology 24
volcanoes 14–15, 77,
78, 102–5, **124–5**
Voyager spacecraft
234, **235**

warning systems
design 7, 13
earthquakes 105
flooding 85
tornados 82, **90–1**
tsunamis 102
volcanoes 105
weather 77, 78–81, 82,
100–1
wilderness survival
140–2, **143–51**
wildfires see fire
Windscale nuclear
incident 56
World Health
Organization (WHO)
31, 63
World War I **27, 29,** 44,
46, 222
World War II **141,** 222

Zimbabwe 17, **61**

Acknowledgments

Thanks to everyone who supported me during the creation of this book, including Dave Clarke, Martin Ball, Graham Taylor, Caroline Kubala, Catriona Melton, Isobel Maclean, Tom Snow, Pete Brittain, Ailsa Clarke, Pete Wylde, Greg Tyler, Amy Burge, Rosanne Taylor, Becky Alexis-Martin, Sarah Harper, John Preston, Terry Andrews, and Alistair McCann. Thanks also to the team at Thames & Hudson – Isabel Jessop, Jane Laing and Tristan de Lancey. Finally, thank you to my parents for their constant support.

The publisher would like to thank Jane Bugaeva, Ruth Ellis, Becky Gee, Helena Lam, Nella Soušková and Mai Suzuki.

About the Author

Taras Young is a researcher with an interest in weird, hidden and forgotten history and culture. He is the author of *Nuclear War in the UK*, an acclaimed visual history of public information materials produced by the British state in preparation for nuclear attack. He has written for a variety of publications, including *History Today*, *BBC History Magazine* and *Fortean Times*.

First published in the United Kingdom in 2022 by Thames & Hudson Ltd, 181A High Holborn, London WC1V 7QX

First published in the United States of America in 2022 by Thames & Hudson Inc, 500 Fifth Avenue, New York, New York, 10110

Apocalypse Ready © 2022 Thames & Hudson Ltd, London

Text © 2022 Taras Young

For image copyright information see pp. 252–253

Designed by Daniel Streat, Visual Fields

British Library Cataloguing-in-Publication Data. A catalogue record for this book is available from the British Library.

Library of Congress Control Number: 2021943338

ISBN 978-0-500-02431-7

Printed and bound in Latvia by Livonia Print

MIX
Paper from
responsible sources
FSC® C002795

Be the first to know about our new releases, exclusive content and author events by visiting
thamesandhudson.com
thamesandhudsonusa.com
thamesandhudson.com.au